MORE THAN WORDS

MORE THAN WORDS

Turn #MeToo into #ISaidSomething

KIRSTEN D. ANDERSON

Editor: Deborah Froese
Cover and Interior Design: Emma Grace

Indigo River Publishing
3 West Garden Street, Ste. 718
Pensacola, FL 32502
www.indigoriverpublishing.com

Ordering Information:
Quantity sales: Special discounts are available on quantity purchases by corporations, associations, and others. For details, contact the publisher at the address above.

Orders by US trade bookstores and wholesalers: Please contact the publisher at the address above.

Printed in the United States of America

Library of Congress Control Number: 2021924105
ISBN: 978-1-954676-25-1

First Edition

The author's former colleagues and bosses are referred to by title, position, or a pseudonym for privacy. Incidents are based upon the author's experience and in some cases, event documentation has been adapted for brevity.

With Indigo River Publishing, you can always expect great books, strong voices, and meaningful messages. Most importantly, you'll always find . . . words worth reading.

This book is dedicated to all those who are searching for more, who crave understanding and yearn for support.

It is an offering of gratitude to each target of sexual harassment who is courageous enough to say something.

TABLE OF CONTENTS

FOREWORD

WHEN KIRSTEN ANDERSON first contacted me regarding a problem she was having at work, there was no way for either of us to know what kind of journey we would take together. As it turned out, the official legal journey took five years, a long time even by justice-system standards. By the time the legal journey finished, my relationship with Kirsten evolved from being her legal adviser to being a friend. In my role as legal adviser and trial Sherpa, my responsibilities ran the spectrum from communications coach and strategist to fashion assistant and cheerleader.

Every lawyer has a path to the profession. While my path to the law was accidental, I was lucky to find great mentors who showed me what a privilege it is to represent people who have suffered the kind of trauma Kirsten Anderson experienced. It is an honor to represent people through the kind of process she writes about in this book, but there is nothing routine about it. Cases like Kirsten's just don't happen every day. Most lawyers aren't lucky enough to work with a client like her or on a case with a set of facts carrying such societal significance. The lucky few who participate in such cases experience the practice of law on an entirely different plain. Rarely do they go to trial.

This book is not a litigation manual. It doesn't explain how to handle or survive cases like Kirsten's. However, it does share what I was lucky enough to learn about Kirsten Anderson over the span of the lawsuit against the state of Iowa: a lawsuit should not define the lawyer or the person they represent, but it often clarifies exactly who they are, bringing out their best and worst qualities. That is precisely what happened in my brief time representing Kirsten.

I was lucky to represent Kirsten not because she listened to my advice, although she did do that, nor because she was a passive bystander in the process. I was lucky to have Kirsten as my client because she embodied my philosophy of life and litigation. People never call the trial lawyer because something wonderful has occurred in their life. They call us when something has happened or is happening to them, and they need help. So, when I talked to Kirsten from the first day until the very end of the lawsuit, my goal was to help her maintain her own sense of who she was and wanted to become. I reminded her often that the litigation could supply a sense of justice, but it could not produce a certain and fair sense of justice. She had to take full responsibility for her life, litigation or not.

That is who she was the first day she wandered into my office and that is who she is today: a bright and curious wife, mother, and daughter. Though the lawsuit and trial that Kirsten writes about in this book did not define her, they did help clarify those qualities. The legal process surely tested those qualities many times, but Kirsten was resolute and ready for whatever result would come.

Lawyers love to tell war stories, tales of heroism and courage in the heat of battle. Funny, those stories always seem to revolve around their own accomplishments. Those are not the interesting stories. The stories I want to hear are like the one you will read in these pages. The nuts and bolts of what happened and how we did it are more interesting coming from the person caught in the eye of the storm. More important than the tales of the process is what we can learn from a person who walked through it, keeping her sense of self and sense of humor along the way. In that sense, this book is for survivors and even those who know, love, and represent them. For it is one thing to espouse a philosophy of life and litigation; it is quite another to actually capture it, live it, and accomplish it.

Thanks, Kirsten for your perseverance, your dedication, for your faith in me, and for continuing to be a bright light to show others the way.

Michael Carroll, March 21, 2021

FOR THOSE WHO FEEL LOST

> It's the 21st Century, yet we are still bemoaning the fact that people are being sexually harassed, bullied, and retaliated against at work. Change is long overdue.

AS YOU READ these words, someone is suffering persecution. 81 percent of females and 43 percent of males have been sexually harassed in their lifetimes.[1] It's affecting their lives and livelihoods. It's paralyzing them. And it's a pervasive problem everyone should care about.

The statistics surprise most people. I hope it angers them, too. It angers me! The global workforce employs way too many jerks with little to no regard for anyone else. They use their positions of power and authority to demean others for personal entertainment or benefit. They compromise workplace integrity, reputation, and financial stability. It isn't right.

The stats referenced—81 percent and 43 percent—are also downright sad and frustrating. Clearly this issue affects everyone directly or indirectly. Unfortunately, most people don't identify sexual harassment, bullying, and retaliation for what it is. They don't understand how such aggression impacts their lives and their ability to contribute to the workplace or the world at large.

I know how damaging these kinds of behaviors can be because I've experienced them. I was once a scared, confused target of sexual harassment and verbal abuse who simply couldn't get over the fact that my coworker and bosses would do and say inappropriate things to a nice girl like me. I shrugged it off, laughed, and even fired back, thinking I needed to prove myself to fit into a male-dominated, locker room-like atmosphere.

My strategic attempts to better fit in and make it stop didn't work. They never do. The harassment I experienced eventually escalated to the point of no return. Everyone in the office knew the environment was damaged. They were afraid to say anything because they knew management would do nothing. They were tired of not being heard, so they gave up.

My story isn't unique. This problem is hiding in plain sight. It lurks in downward glances, whispers, and gossip. It hangs around water coolers, locker rooms, and board rooms. It creeps into comments that make you blush or feel uncomfortable, yet if the aggression isn't directed toward you, you feel it isn't your problem.

I'm here to tell you that it very much is your problem. It's everyone's problem. Do not look the other way. Do not walk away, and do not say nothing. If you want safe, healthy, productive workplaces, it's time to step up and invest in yourself and those around you. You can do it. The concepts in this book show you how. They aren't radical, nor are they complex, but they will challenge you to adjust your perspective.

We live in an imperfect world hell-bent on perfection, yet stuck on status quo. Our TV shows portray a societal ideal that is hardly realistic. Cultural imagery projects perfection in all sorts of ways. Magazine covers are littered with airbrushed models whose flawless bodies don't reflect the average human form. Social media "influencers" show only a tiny peek into their lives—just what they want us to see. The "effortless" photograph really took hours to set up and touch up. It's imagery management and it's all fake—quite the opposite of perfect.

Even the regulations our country's workplaces abide by are far from perfect. When it comes to labor and employment, federal laws are interpreted broadly. There is little uniformity from state to state, which means keeping track of labor and employment laws regarding workplace harassment is a job in and of itself. Many state laws are vague, difficult to interpret, and behind the times. They are reactionary at best.

American society has only recently begun to test discussions about subjects like gender and non-conformity, pay equity, equality at work, family leave, and what all those things mean. Establishing a comfortable attitude toward such conversations takes time and effort. Because of the high level of commitment required, many workplaces resist. They won't change. They're stuck in the past, in a time when the world belonged to the "good ol' boys club." In that world, equality and respect are laughable afterthoughts. Think of breakroom walls adorned with calendars of bare-chested women. Some workplaces are threatened by change. Why change what has seemingly worked forever?

I want others to care about this pervasive problem. I want them to understand the complexities of harassment and abuse. Public reports don't show the full picture, and targets of harassment deserve to have the full picture revealed. Not everyone has experienced demoralizing behavior that causes them to feel less than, marginalized, or put down, and that makes the full implications hard to grasp. That's why I'm committed to creating enlightenment through education. I tell anyone who will listen that my mission is to end workplace harassment in my lifetime. Harassment isn't a joke. It's no joke because the consequences, as I will explain in later chapters, are deadly serious. Personal, professional, and financial consequences result from ignoring the problems of harassment, bullying, and retaliation in the workplace.

I am outraged, saddened, and exasperated to know that there are others all over the country who have experienced or are still enduring the ugliness that I went through. You won't find these people in the head-lines or on television crying about their situation. They may work at gas stations, on assembly lines, or on night shift cleaning crews. They work in offices across every state. They are your neighbors, your cousins, your former co-workers. Their victimization happened in the cubicle next to yours and you may not have even noticed.

Merely talking about this issue is tiresome, so this book does more than lead lunchtime discussion or roundtable chit-chat during break. This book is actionable. It's the 21st century, yet we are still bemoaning the fact that people are being sexually harassed, bullied, and retaliated against at work. Change is long overdue.

A constant stream of people who have been through terrible situations reach out to me. The number one question they ask is how to go about choosing a lawyer. But they also ask a handful of other practical questions:

1. How do I tell if I'm being harassed/bullied/retaliated against?

2. How can I hold my harasser/organization accountable?

3. How will I support my family if I leave or have been fired from my job?

4. How can I make a difference in the world and ensure this doesn't happen to someone else?

This book will answer all those questions.

People who reach out to me also want reassurance and a return to happiness, but that's harder to address. Happiness is quite personal and how to get there is different for everyone. In *More than Words: Turn #MeToo into #ISaidSomething*, I share what helped me. I recovered from a deep, dark pit of mental anguish to revive my spirit and create a posi-tive outlook on life. Perhaps my journey will provide some ideas for you.

This book isn't simply for those who have been abused, however. It's for family members who struggle to understand what their loved one is going through. It's for co-workers who witnessed a disturbing, awkward, or embarrassing episode and didn't know what to say in the moment, so said nothing. Time passed and others moved on, but the moment haunts them.

This book is also for the jerk who commented in a group meeting about a co-worker's sexual preferences—all for a laugh—and now realizes it was in bad taste.

More than Words is about gaining the knowledge and understanding necessary to create a better world. Keep these questions in the back of your mind while you read this book:

- How are you treating others?

- How are you investing in and showing up for yourself?

- What words and deeds are you putting out in the world? Would you say or do them to your mother? No? Then do not say or do it. At all. Ever. To anyone.

- Are you comfortable with intervention and confrontation if the situation requires it?

Each chapter in *More Than Words* includes a "Think About It" section prompting reflection on the chapter content. Chapters 1 through 11 each conclude with a fictional case study that paints a picture of sexual harassment, bullying, and retaliation in the modern workplace. These case studies are drawn from the many stories of people who reached out to me for guidance and solace. Designed to provoke emotional responses, they also challenge thought and action through a series of "Assess the Situation" questions that allow you to consider how you might respond in a similar situation.

This book will make you think, but above all, it is a friendly reminder to people everywhere: love yourself, relish your strength and capabilities as they are, and stop trying to achieve perfection. Rather, focus on your ongoing journey toward improvement, to becoming a better, stronger, more accomplished person.

We must encourage one another and accept each other as we are. We don't tell each other often enough how much we appreciate each other. We don't tell each other how much we value and respect one another. This validation is especially needed by those who engage in thankless jobs for many different reasons. Without validation, it's easy to feel a bit lost.

For those who *do* feel lost right now: you are not alone. Others care about you and want success for you.

For those who feel unappreciated: know you *are* valued. The frustration, emptiness and loneliness that accompanies that feeling of being unappreciated passes. Taking action helps—action in movement and exercise, action toward self-care, and action as an agent of change.

For those who feel low, thought you were alone, cried out for help, and toughed it out: know that what you are experiencing is normal. You may feel off-balance and out of whack right now, but you will find your center again.

I have experienced all of these lows. It does get better. Know that you are enough as you are right now. You are amazingly unique, respected, and valued. Don't forget it. And don't forget to tell someone else how much they mean to you. Empower them to stand up to the jerks they encounter.

Although there are plenty of nasty people in the world, I'm optimistic that "jerks" are a dying breed. Through the power of education, enlightenment, and a collective mindset coupled with accountability and consequences, jerks will become extinct. Workplace environments will become safer, more productive, and engaging. Instead of stirring fear and angst, the workplace will become a place to simply do work.

CHAPTER 1

MORE THAN A VICTIM

> Even when I was being sexually harassed and at my lowest point both mentally and physically, I would never have admitted to being a victim. I didn't feel weak or oppressed.

I HAD NEVER been as nervous as I was on the morning I took the stand in my civil suit against the State of Iowa, my former employer. My choice of clothes seemed small in the scheme of things, but I knew that appearances made a difference in perception, especially in a court of law. I dressed in a plain charcoal-colored suit with white, button-down shirt, black dress shoes, and minimal jewelry—nothing to distract the jury from me and my story. I stopped in the bathroom to collect myself and savor a moment of prayer before entering the courtroom as I had done every day of the trial.

I looked in the mirror and forced myself to take two deep breaths and exhale slowly. Sweat beaded through my makeup. A rollercoaster of emotions swept through me and tumbled into underlying anxiety, nervousness, and fear before barreling toward anticipated embarrassment, guilt, and shame. The ride would end with an overwhelming desire to be understood and believed. I had to help the jury see me and hear my voice.

On this day, I knew what awaited me in the courtroom: tough questions and admittance of being a person I didn't like. A person I had tried to forget and was ashamed of. A person riddled with guilt who did what she had to in order to keep her job.

The county courthouse bathroom I stood in wasn't nice, but it wasn't awful either. In that moment, it served as my sanctuary. It held two stalls and an old, sagging couch. The mirror, still intact, had chipped edges and reflected the image of an anxious wreck. I had to calm that image down before I returned to the court room where I was suing my employer for wrongful termination, sexual harassment, and retaliation—all because I complained about sexual harassment and a toxic work environment.

I needed the jury to know I wasn't simply some pushover who allowed myself to be verbally abused over and over again. I was a fighter standing up for what's right. I was more than a victim. I was a person with hobbies, dreams, goals, friends, and high moral and ethical standards. That all changed after working for five years in a toxic environment. I had changed.

I didn't want the fight, but I was ready for the battle arena. Because it was a battle. The toughest one of my life. My lawyer, Michael Carroll, told me it would be hard, but he prepared me to face it. My case revolved around proving that the environment I had worked within for five years was toxic, and that I had been subject to ongoing objectively and subjectively offensive behavior by those in a position of power. Four years and countless hours of gathering evidence, filing paperwork, and taking witness testimony had built to this moment.

Earlier in the week, my former co-workers and bosses testified about their experiences in the statehouse. They talked about me, my character, and my work—all of which had deteriorated over time as continuous sexual harassment, bullying, and retaliatory behavior was doled out to me.

Now it was my turn to be heard. I pushed the bathroom door open and stepped into the courthouse hallway, navigating through the hustle and bustle of people arriving for traffic and small claims court or reporting for jury duty. I longed for the comfort of the friendly faces of my lawyers.

CHARACTER ON TRIAL

The court allowed minimal media presence at the trial, and the local NBC television affiliate won the bid to broadcast live proceedings. Many friends near and far—and people I didn't know—were watching the live feed from the courtroom. This real-time scrutiny was almost paralyzing. Things I hadn't even told my husband would be admitted for other people to hear. My deep, dark feelings, my depression, my anxiety, my strained marriage, my participation in inappropriate behavior; it would all be on the record.

The newspaper, *The Des Moines Register*, was also allowed in the courtroom to cover the proceedings. My parents attended the trial almost daily, missing only one day each. The courtroom wasn't packed, even though it was open to the public. I noticed a few young people dressed in business attire taking notes—law students—and some strangers, but otherwise the courtroom was quiet and sparsely populated.

The previous evening, I had worked late with my lawyer to review lines of questioning and practice my answers. I knew the defense attorneys would try to chip away at my character. They would try to make me doubt my own experiences by questioning me sternly. It was their job to do that. I saw how they handled previous witnesses and how they handled taking my original deposition. It was uncomfortable. I didn't want to share embarrassing experiences like jokes about my sex life, but it all needed to come out and be entered into the court transcript.

I was nervous beyond words.

The judge called me to the stand as a witness, and the court clerk swore me in. Mike, my lawyer, started questioning me as we had discussed the night before. I told my side of the story, how I had been sexually harassed for years, and after complaining, I was pushed out of my job when my boss no longer wanted to deal with my insistent pursuit of a harassment-free environment.

Sweat poured through my white cotton blouse, and I wondered if my suit jacket would hold up for the next few hours.

Mike gave me a reassuring nod. "Let's talk a little bit more about the office environment. Would you say that the office environment when you worked there at the caucus was generally collegial?"

"From time to time, yes." I resisted the urge to clear my throat.

"And when you work long hours in a small office, you get to know each other well?"

"Yes." Keep your answers short, Mike had told me.

"There were jokes in the staff office?"

"There were lots of jokes."

Mike continued that line of questioning to reveal that the barrage of jokes occurred in person and by email, and that Al was one of the people who often joked around.

"Did he sometimes take his jokes too far?

"Yes."

"And did he do that with both men and women?"

"He did." I braced myself. I knew what question was coming next.

"Did you yourself sometimes joke around?" Mike asked, matter-of-factly.

"Yes."

The questions became more personal, digging at my spirit. Mike gently coaxed the confessions out of me: I joked with Al in person. I joked by e-mail. I raised my voice to Al, and I used foul language in the office. My cheeks burned with shame as well as defiance. The office atmosphere had punched me so often that it had reduced me to this state.

Mike drew his questioning to a close. "Kirsten, you testified at some length yesterday and again today about your work experiences in the Senate Republican Caucus. The work environment you testified about was from time to time very unwelcome. What was the price of working in the 'boys club'?"

My chest tightened. I knew Mike was going to ask this question, just as we had practiced. I knew how important my answer was to the jury. I drew a deep breath. "I felt it was steep. The price for admittance was steep. In fact, I compromised my integrity from time to time. I didn't act like myself from time to time. And it was because I wanted these men in the Senate to like me and to respect me. And that's not right. I think about that a lot. A lot. That was the price."

"In the end, what was it, if anything, that allowed you to stand up?"

"My strong values and ultimately my integrity."

"Do you believe on those occasions in which you complained to your bosses up to and including May 17, 2013, you were exercising your values and your integrity?"

"Yes." My reply sounded confident.

"In your complaints in 2010 and 2012 and ultimately your complaint on May 17, 2013, what gave you the strength to do that?"

"A couple things," I replied. I referred to my friend and coworker—whom I'll call Jan—and the fact that I was a mother. "I have a son. I would never allow him to say these things to other people. I don't want to raise him that way. And with that in mind, that's why I made the complaint, the original complaint." The court took a lunch recess in the midst of my testimony, and I left the courthouse to get some air. I walked across the street to a market that had a deli counter where I ordered a sandwich. The woman in line in front of me turned around as I waited on my order and said with a genuine smile, "I really like your hair. You look very nice."

I was taken off-guard because I was so deep in thought and exhausted from sharing such raw emotions on the witness stand all morning. "Thank you," I responded. "I appreciate that because I don't feel like I look good today."

"Well, you do look nice." She emphasized her words with a smile.

The afternoon would be the final stretch of the rollercoaster ride with defense attorneys cross-examining me, firing more of the same demeaning and hard-to-answer questions my way. All of this weighed heavily on me in that moment. The fact that someone, a stranger, had acknowledged me in a moment of such darkness was the sign I needed. She saw me. She saw more than my pain and angst and looked past it. She went out of her way to pay me a simple compliment. It made me feel like more than just a target of harassment.

I snapped back to life and gobbled down my sandwich before marching back to the courthouse.

My afternoon testimony was just as rough as I had anticipated. The defense attorney made me read emails I sent to other coworkers to prove that I'd participated in the bad behavior I was complaining about. Reading those emails out loud to the jury was mortifying, yet they proved that I had become so jaded and frustrated over years of working in a toxic environment that I was participating in the behavior I was trying to end.

Some emails were typical office gripes about people, and some were catty. I made fun of my boss—the staff director—and mocked his inflated ego. A few emails were off-color jokes that I wasn't proud of sending but I sent them anyway. Everyone in my office was doing it. I wanted people to laugh at what I sent. I wanted to be included, to be in on the joke. All of those distasteful messages were reminders that I had devolved into a person I did not want to be. Someone who liked to go along to get along. Someone who was tired of protesting and saying, "Knock it off." That's what workplace harassment does to a person: it turns them into someone else so they can survive the persecution.

The defense lawyers tried to make it look as though I was participating in the lewd behavior and therefore, that I encouraged and supported it. I certainly did not, but they only cared that I sent vulgar emails from my work account.

The questions from the defense kept coming. As I described the toll on my marriage and my ability to mother my son, tears crept down my cheeks. All I could think about was my flawed humanness and how all the people in this courtroom were there because I made them be there. I made them hear details about uncomfortable things. The ridiculousness of the situation hit me hard. The choice I made to stand up for what's right hit me hard. For years, I was yelled at, cussed out, shown porn, laughed at, called names, and had my sex life and body parts scrutinized. Now I was being forced to defend myself on the witness stand where I not only had to shine a light on the embarrassing inappropriateness I experienced, but on my own descent into cattiness as a defensive response to the situation. It didn't seem fair. I felt immense shame and guilt for my intermittent participation and now I was being embarrassed yet again, in a different way, by someone who didn't really know me or know what I had been through.

VANQUISH NEGATIVE CONNOTATIONS

I loathe the word *victim* because it carries a negative connotation associated with weakness and oppression. *Weak* never felt appropriate to me or my identity, and it doesn't reflect what I'm now trying to teach others. Even when I was being sexually harassed and at my lowest point both mentally and physically, I would never have admitted to being a victim. I didn't feel weak or oppressed. I had been raised as a strong, empowered woman, yet I was being consumed by a toxic workplace culture.

So-called victims are too often boxed and categorized. People think they know us and pass judgement on us, but they cannot, should not, do so. Any human being is more complex than any one judgement, thought or perception. I want to flip the script on the way we view people who suffer harassment by finding an alternative word for *victim*. They are—we are—more than that.

We are more than what you read about in the news.

We have families, friends, hopes, dreams, plans for the future.

We are passionate people who care deeply about others.

Reading something about us doesn't mean you know us. Keep your judgements to yourself.

We have stories we would like to tell from our own perspectives.

We have thoughts and opinions that will resonate with some and surprise others.

We have a tribe that cares about us and wants us to succeed.

We enjoy privacy and we don't want to be labelled.

We know there are others like us out there. Far too many others.

There has to be a better word than *victim*. The synonyms are no better and there are hundreds of them, like *prey*, *hunted*, *wretch*, *sacrifice*, and *martyr* to name a few.

The word victim has Latin origins (*victima*) dating back to the 15th Century. It means "one that is injured, destroyed, or sacrificed under any of various conditions."[2] It takes my breath away to think that I was purposefully injured and sacrificed as a victim of sexual harassment. That I had to be fired from my job for someone else to benefit in some way. To think that anyone is sacrificed, or their spirit figuratively killed for another to succeed, makes my blood boil.

Let's change the vernacular. Let's use stronger terminology that doesn't leave people feeling powerless. Let's use the word *target*, a term that has been tossed around empowerment circles that means "a person, object, or place selected as the aim of an attack."[3]

Targets aren't relegated to the Hollywood elite disrespected by highly-paid executives who inappropriately crossed the line. Targets come from all walks of life and from all types of positions. They are doctors, students, waitresses, clerks, dental hygienists, grocers, young, old, wealthy, poor. Targets are people struggling to find their voice. They're considering whether or not coming forward would ruin their reputation, isolate them from their friends, or get them fired Many targets bravely share with me their stories, their truths. Some even put their careers on the line to do so. Ultimately, targets of workplace harassment want validation—validation that what happened to them was in fact wrong and inappropriate. Like me, they want to create change, not only for themselves, but for others.

Don't treat targets differently than anyone else unless they ask you to, and don't feel sorry for them. Instead, simply consider the fact that they're going through something you know nothing about. The best way to help a target is by withholding judgement, offering support, and being an upright bystander who provides intervention if inappropriate behavior occurs.

LIFE AS A TARGET BEGINS

I became a target within a few months of taking a job as communications director within the Iowa Legislature. During a break in evening debate, I went to dinner with a senator and a man I'll call Al Schuster, a legislative analyst. Al was a tall, middle-aged man who deployed swear words like salt on French fries. What I thought would be a meal comprised of small talk between bites of burger turned into an embarrassing and awkward situation.

"Tell me what your wife does, Senator?" I asked.

"She's working and taking care of the kids while I'm here. Four days a week is enough time away, and she says she misses me when I'm at the capitol."

"Missing you? My wife misses me, and I live here," Al piped in. "My wife can't get enough of me. She is so amorous. Last night, I think we went three rounds before I wore her out."

"Wow, Al, that's something. My wife isn't what you'd call 'amorous' but we get it done—you know what I mean."

"We changed the subject quickly!" I declared. "I just wanted to know more about the senator's family."

"Well, now you know," said Al. "What about you, Kirsten. Is your manly husband amorous? How many times do you get it on?"

"I don't kiss and tell, and I won't share that with you," I said.

Initially, I didn't think of Al's crude remarks and coarse language as harassment. Al was just a jerk being a jerk. Everyone else nervously laughed and made excuses for his behavior. Perhaps they were just used to him; he had been around state politics a long time, and he was valued because he got things done.

I didn't step up right away either. I was naïve and wanted to get ahead in my career. Like the others, I often went along Al's unsettling behavior, ignored it, or voiced a mild protest. Eventually, going along broke me down. I couldn't do it anymore. I was tired of not being heard or taken seriously. Tired of being laughed at or hearing replies like, "Ah, you're funny," or "You've heard worse," or "Give it a rest. You women are all the same."

Raising my voice fell literally and figuratively on deaf ears. Eventually, I came to realize that no one wanted anything to change. No one cared about me, my work, or my opinion. If you've ever been harassed, you'll relate. You begin to realize that you're a token in some way. You're different or outside the "norm" of the work environment. You might be a brain who is taken advantage of to raise the level of everyone else's work product. Or you might be female in a male-dominated office like me: a woman viewed as arm candy for someone else.

Apparently, that's what I was hired for, although I didn't learn about it until years later. My co-worker, Jan, confided that the senate leader who hired me would say of me proudly, "I've got my girl now."

"Are you kidding me?" I asked.

"Kirsten, he wanted to pad his ego and have an attractive woman follow him around the Capitol, hanging on his every word," Jan said. "Not that you aren't qualified for your job, but you're also *that* girl."

I was initially shocked, but in the midst of a toxic environment, it became less surprising daily.

CHANGED BY TOXICITY

Being a target means you gradually change. You change your behavior to survive the environment, and that forces a change in your self-perception, usually negative. Lawyers deemed my work environment "severe and pervasive," ripe with objectively and subjectively inappropriate behavior that went unchecked for years.

My co-worker, Al, freely shared his thoughts about women's body parts. "Check out the ass on that lady," he'd say, pointing to a woman walking by the office window. He'd brag about rubbing up a female co-worker's breasts as he made rude hand gestures.

"Everyone knows she slept with the entire baseball team back in the day," he said of a female senator. "She's what you call 'loose.'"

A male senator I worked for laughed.

I inserted myself into the conversation from across the room. "Oh, c'mon, Al, you don't know that. Don't say that."

All eyes looked at me.

"I do know it. I went to the same school she did." Al's tone and expression implied he couldn't believe I was actually questioning him. He and the male senator in the room burst into laughter.

Al also made a lot of derogatory statements about homosexuals, African Americans, Asian Americans, Mexicans, and Mexican Americans. He tacked newspaper articles all over his cubicle wall about crimes committed by various ethnic groups and would tell us, in colorful language, why those groups did not deserve to be in the United States or worse, why they should be wiped off the face of the earth.

My co-workers and I were not off limits to Al's teasing. Many days we found ourselves the butt of his sexual jokes and insinuations. He would go out of his way to make us feel uncomfortable by turning many tame conversations into sexual ones.

"Going for a little pickle tickle at lunch with your hubby?"

In 2010, Al was in the midst of ending a long relationship in his personal life and taking it out on his co-workers. His jokes and insinuations increased. The atmosphere became tense, stressful, and at times, unbearable. Al seemed bent on instilling fear and he didn't seem to care what we thought about it. Our staff director at that time was usually in his office or another area of the building where he couldn't respond to Al's antics. Al carried on unchecked for so long that he became untouchable.

After one long and loud tirade of his derogatory views of women, I couldn't stay silent any longer. I somehow convinced Jan that we should complain together to the staff director.

I asked Jan to step out of the office and into the public cafeteria area of the Capital where we could have a discussion away from our other co-workers.

"Jan, I can't take any more of Al's rants. He called his ex and every woman the *C* word just now!"

"I know. His rants have escalated since the breakup," Jan pointed out.

"I'm fed up and he isn't listening to any of us. I think we need to say something to the staff director," I said.

"I've seen how this ends and I don't think it will make a difference anyway. The staff director hasn't done anything about Al before." Jan explained that Al had been a problem for years before I started working there. Most of the staff—all males—laughed along with Al. Many of the senators participated in his jokes.

"Look," I said. "I'm going to talk to the staff director, and I'd like you with me. Strength in numbers. I'll do all the talking."

We went to the staff director, and I did all the talking. Jan confirmed my story.

What followed was the quietest week experienced in some time. Then one morning, Al stormed into the office and roared, "You women are all such bitches! I won't stay quiet on this one."

No one dared make a peep or ask a question for fear of launching another tirade. Al sat at his desk and powered up his computer to a silent room. Everyone just went on with the day.

Unfortunately, Al's hostile announcement signaled that he was starting up again and didn't care how we responded. We later found out that the staff director had not filed any paperwork or sought council from higher-ups after I issued my complaint. There was zero paper trail. We had no idea if any consequences were demanded or if any reprimand took place. It didn't matter because it didn't put an end to things; it merely put them on pause for a time.

Ultimately, I hit multiple breaking points and I complained in 2011 and 2012. My complaints went nowhere, and life went on as usual in the office. And then Al launched another joke that changed everything.

It was December 2012. Our new chief advisor—let's call him Goldman—held an all-staff meeting. Goldman was the kind of man who entered any room and commanded it—fancy clothes, expensive shoes, and a loud voice. He generally set the tone for meetings and seemed used to being the funniest person in attendance. That day, however, before Goldman had a chance to set the tone, Al goaded the entire staff to attention with a crude joke. He told us that a potential clerk was qualified for the position because "she likes the rhythm."

He smiled, waiting for a response. As if on cue, the staff chorused, "What does that mean?"

He replied in a matter-of-fact voice with a punchline that made me sick: "She likes black dick." As if this was a prerequisite for any administrative job.

No one laughed but Al. The statement sucked the air out of the room as we all waited to see what Goldman's reaction would be. We were used to Al's behavior, but how would a new boss react? As Al laughed, Goldman bristled. A look of confusion crossed his face. He said something to the effect of *don't say that again*, and left the room, lightning fast.

Goldman singled out me and Jan, making us come into his office to provide a statement about the incident and outline the ongoing issue. Both Jan and I wanted the behavior to end, and Goldman assured us it would. This marked my third complaint and a distinctive turning point. The staff director suddenly began giving me bad reviews and calling my work "substandard." He also put me on a performance improvement plan. His tone and demeanor toward me changed. He became combative and confrontational toward me. I got used to being called into his office for simply doing my job.

Frustrated, I made one last-ditch effort to initiate change and submitted my fourth complaint on May 17, 2013. I wrote a well-thought-out memo detailing the harassment and abuse I had suffered for years. I was fired seven hours later.

Just over a month before my case against the State of Iowa went to trial, I sent a memo to my lawyer painting a picture of how being a target had changed me. I wanted to negate the stigma of being a target and give flight to my own voice. It was never an official court document, but it was cathartic in my personal healing process. Here is the gist of that memo:

I know who I was and how I lost my way. My husband, Jeff, has said I'm not the same person he married, and it makes me sad. The firing event changed my life, and I feel like I will always have a mental scar.

I was confident, strong-willed, even more outgoing than I am now, ambitious, up for lively debate, and ready to take on people who tried to prove me wrong.

Now, I constantly question my worth and my work product. I second-guess decisions and how they will affect me, my family, and my career. I battle depression, take medication, and truly want to go to therapy regularly but can't afford it. I cry frequently in front of my son and snap at him too quickly because sometimes the little things are stressful to me. They didn't used to be.

I worry that my husband will be disappointed in me. Sometimes I don't even tell him things because I'm worried of what he'll think or that he'll say I need to toughen up. That he'll see my insecurities and indecisiveness and bring to light my overly sensitive nature and deem them to be way too weak.

I feel like a dog who has been beaten down—an animal whose young spirit was broken and has become complacent. I don't want to feel that way, and I don't want to show that defeat to my son. It's so hard to get out of that mindset. I put so much importance and hope in my career and it was all shattered. It's hard to put on a confident attitude and hard to not show the anxiety I'm experiencing. I'm constantly paranoid that people I encounter will know who I am from the news of my "scandal." I'm continuously worried that my work will be picked apart to the point of humiliation and embarrassment. I'm way too worried about what other people think of me and my work. I shouldn't feel such deep shame about standing up for what's right.

I was on an upwardly mobile path, ready to lead others, and then my confidence was shattered. I question that path now, and it makes me mad. I feel like it was taken away from me by an organization I trusted.

I hold the legislative process in high regard. It's fascinating and democracy is a fantastic thing that we have in place in this wonderful coun-

try. I loved learning about politics and civic engagement in high school and college. I loved it so much that I minored in political science and after college worked for a US Senator. Elected officials have power. They work for the American people. They should be protecting them. They should, through government, help make peoples' lives better.

Now I feel like my naïve, rose-colored glasses are off. At the state level, elected officials are part-time hacks with little experience. They're control freaks who communicate poorly, don't deal well with others, and don't care about the people right in front of them, working for them. Human resource issues and harassment are things they don't understand, care about, or want to deal with. How disappointing.

Harassment should never happen anywhere and especially in the halls of the Statehouse, where we hold elected officials to a higher standard; where politicians make the laws that Iowans abide by—the laws that keep citizens safe. The treatment I received is a violation against all Iowans.

At the time, I was embarrassed to reveal personal and intimate thoughts and feelings, but writing the memo ended up being therapeutic for me. I had felt alone for such a long time. Alone in what I went through, and alone in my road to recovery. I wanted someone to understand my perspective. I wanted a return to normalcy, but I did not want to minimize or forget the significance of what had occurred.

By the time I wrote that memo, Mike had been my lawyer for a few years. We had grown close as we worked on my case. Although he knew my story, he asked for a no-holds-barred depiction of my life after being fired in an effort to help him do his work. Looking back, I know what I laid out was honest and not unusual for the circumstances. I hope others read it and see the same. The process of writing that memo helped me work toward my new normal.

THINK ABOUT IT

- People who are sexually harassed are more than weak, oppressed victims; they are targets. Try using *target* as a more appropriate term.

- Some targets may not realize they are in toxic situations. Education, enlightenment, and support are keys to understanding.

- Never underestimate the power of a smile or a basic compliment. Making eye contact with the person you are communicating with is huge and important. It's a respectful gesture linked to recognition and it matters.

- Everyone should know the feeling of mattering. Everyone matters. You matter.

PUT IT TO WORK: SHELBY AND THE COLLEGE DREAM

Shelby recently turned eighteen and graduated from high school. For the past two summers, she's worked at the auto body shop where her father is a mechanic. She answers the phone, processes payments, and schedules appointments. In Shelby's eyes, it's a great job with good pay for a teenager with a laser-like focus on earning money toward her college education which begins in the fall. If she can finish college, she will be the first in her family to do so.

Timid and self-conscious, Shelby stays out of everyone's way and does not often go into the break room. As the only female at the shop, she feels uncomfortable trying to make conversation with a room full of male mechanics.

Shelby's boss, Roger, owns the business. His office is right behind Shelby's desk. He frequently checks on her and answers questions or helps with various issues that arise. Roger typically stands behind Shelby and gently rubs her shoulders or neck while they converse. Shelby is extremely uncomfortable with his behavior, but she has no idea how to respond. Typically, she shrugs away or pushes his hand off while chatting nervously. Sometimes it works. Other times it does not. She started wearing baggy clothing to draw attention away from her body, hoping Roger will lose any interest in touching her.

Not long ago, Shelby ran into some problems with the credit card processing system. She had to call Roger from his office to help. Roger pulled up a chair next to Shelby's and placed a hand on her upper thigh as he walked her through the troubleshooting process. On another occasion, she was called into Roger's office to learn the new scheduling tool. Roger invited her to sit on his lap. Terrified and unsure how to refuse, Shelby complied. She learned the tool as quickly as possible and returned to her desk.

Last week, Roger began asking Shelby for hugs at the end of her shift. As he hugs Shelby, he moves his hands up and down her back and sometimes puts his hand under her shirt. Shelby is terrified. She does not want this attention, but she doesn't know what to say or how to stop it. She's fearful of what might happen, and she does not want to jeopardize her father's position in the shop. She does not want to lose her recent pay increase because that could jeopardize her college education.

Occasionally, Shelby and her father will discuss work over dinner at home. Shelby has tried to find the right opportunity to mention Roger's inappropriateness to her father but has not yet found the courage.

ASSESS THE SITUATION

- What can Shelby do to stop Roger's inappropriate behavior?
- What might happen if Shelby says and does nothing?
- How can Shelby find the courage to say something?
- What conversations can we have with young workers about the workplace?
- How can we have constructive conversations with colleagues we don't know well?
- How can we help workers avoid feeling isolated and alone?

CHAPTER 2

PIVOTAL MOMENTS
AND TOUGH DECISIONS

> May 17, 2013 changed my life in more ways than I can count. It set me on a journey that led to serious soul searching. It also prompted me to go out into the world and make change the best way I know how—through education.

RECOGNIZING THE DEFINING moments in our lives helps us move forward productively. My termination was a defining moment for me. I replay the events of that day when I need confirmation of growth and how far I have come. It's an exercise in strength, maturity, professionalism, and confidence—all wonderful things I'm proud of. I don't recount the day to wallow in self-righteousness but rather to focus on lessons learned in the hopes it inspires others.

I felt good on the fateful morning of Friday, May 17, 2013. I had decided things in my life needed to improve, and it would start by asking for change in the workplace. I was optimistic about going into work that day which was a welcome and long forgotten feeling. For far too long, I'd been living in fear about what mean and degrading thing would be said to me at work.

I chose to wear a bright blue skirt with a ruffle at the hem and a basic orange cotton sweater that morning to represent strength and confidence. I didn't want to dress in something drab that would allow me to sink into the background. I wanted to be seen at a time when I had been relegated to the background, pushed off, verbally abused, and lashed out at over my so-called incompetency—something that had never occurred before I began complaining about the toxic work environment.

I strode into the staff director's office and confidently handed him the memo I had typed up the night before. "I want you to read this," I said. He didn't take notice of me, so I retreated to my cubicle. I knew he couldn't do anything before conferring with Chief Advisor Goldman anyway, so I would simply have to wait for him to respond or ask him for an explanation later.

Back at my desk, I acclimatized to the day. Fridays were busy because senators typically returned home for the weekends, and that gave staff a chance to catch up on work we couldn't get to earlier in the week due to legislative proceedings. With the memo top of mind, I worried about my ability to focus for the day. I was on high alert. The staff director or Goldman could call me at any moment to address my concerns. The deafening silence was interrupted only by the staff director's door opening and slamming closed all day long.

THE MOMENT THINGS CHANGED

Everything had come to a head a couple of nights earlier when my husband overheard a cellphone conversation at 10:00 p.m. as we were getting ready for bed.

I picked up my ringing phone from my bedside nightstand. "This is Kirsten," I said.

"What the hell were you thinking today?" a loud voice thundered in response. It was Chief Advisor Goldman. He, like the staff director, had turned on me after my third complaint about Al, a particularly sharp sting because Goldman had witnessed Al's abhorrent "black dick" joke with obvious shock. He knew about Al's behavior, and he told Jan and I it wouldn't happen again. Now, Goldman was on the attack. "We aren't getting any press coverage tonight on the information you sent out." He was referring to a press release and documentation about a senator who was participating in an ethics investigation, papers he had asked me to fax to all the news outlets that afternoon.

Why he had wanted me to use the fax instead of email was baffling enough in to begin with—the fax machine had been collecting dust for years—but the fact that he was calling at 10:00 p.m. to berate me was something new and disturbing.

"I don't know what to tell you. I did exactly what you told me to do. I can't force the media to run our story," I replied angrily. I was tired and just wanted to go to bed.

"Your stupidity is costing us coverage," he shouted. "There isn't even a blurb on any station! Did you fax every single page of the documentation?"

"I did!" I had even questioned if I should be touching the documentation. The evidence Goldman wanted me to use was technically not state-sanctioned work. It was campaign material that state employees were strictly forbidden to handle, and his demand that I send it felt like a ludicrous display of his power over me.

"Get back into the office NOW and refax it! Fix your fucking mistake, you idiot."

My cheeks burned with humiliation and anger. "Right now? It's just after ten and the newscast will be over by the time I get in there. The news cycle is over for the day." I hissed into the phone. I did not want to go back to the office so late, by myself.

"Yes, NOW—did I stutter? I'll meet you in the office to make sure you do it right."

"OK," I said as tears welled up in my eyes. I hung up the phone.

"What was that?" Jeff sat up in bed, looking shocked and concerned. "I could hear him clear over here yelling at you. What's he want you to do? Does he always talk to you that way?"

"I have to go into the office now and fix a mistake Goldman said I made today when I was dealing with that ethics investigation I told you about."

"Right now? It's so late, and that side of town isn't the safest after dark."

"Yes, now. And he said he'd meet me there, so I have to go." I stood there for a moment, phone in hand. Then I started wandering around the room in a state of shocked confusion. What would happen next?

"Ok, calm down," Jeff said, worry rising in his voice. "What's going on and why would anyone have to fix anything so late at night?"

And then my story gushed out. I told Jeff how my bosses—the staff director and Goldman— started making work difficult for me after I had complained about Al's ongoing behavior. I told him how they continually yelled at me, called me names, and heavily scrutinized my work.

"Honey, that's retaliation and it's illegal. Why didn't you tell me about this?"

"I thought I could handle it," I sobbed.

"Clearly you can't," he observed. "You better get to the office now because you don't want to give him any more ammo to fire you, but tomorrow, we discuss your options and how to get you out of this. No wonder you've been on edge and snapping at me so much."

A weight had suddenly been lifted from my shoulders. By not wanting to burden my husband, I put pressure on him in other ways without realizing it. His recognition and understanding made me feel less alone and stronger. After we hashed things out the next day, Jeff encouraged me to call a lawyer.

THE LEGAL PROCESS BEGINS

On Thursday, May 16, 2013, I called attorney Michael Carroll for the first time. A friend recommended I talk to Mike. He knew Mike to be fair, reasonable above all else, and caring in how he worked with clients.

Mike immediately put me at ease. "I think you should come see me right now. Today. Can you do that?" he asked.

"Right now? I was actually trying to set up an appointment for later," I said. "I need to go get my son from daycare."

"I think you should come see me today. From the few things you've said and the office you work in, it would be good for me to go over some things for your benefit. It will give you piece of mind. I also want to fully understand your story and what you're experiencing."

I don't remember exactly what I told Mike that warranted his sense of urgency. It might have been the sound of my voice, or maybe he sensed I was on the verge of tears through the entire brief conversation, or perhaps the disgusting nature of the incidents I described sounded an alarm. At his urging, I arranged for my husband to pick up our son. I went to Mike's office immediately after work feeling terrified, anxious, and relieved all at the same time. I needed a lawyer with kid gloves, and I was equally sure he'd have them and concerned he wouldn't. I was in a deplorable mental state. I lacked self-confidence and cried at the drop of a hat. I was consumed by fear of what would happen to me at work, essentially reduced to such a shell of my former self that others were noticing, including my family.

Mike greeted me at his office door in a pair of jeans and a long-sleeved t-shirt. With a relaxed and calming manner, he looked me in the eye, asked questions about my feelings and about the facts of my situation. I immediately felt respected, which is something I hadn't experienced in a long time. I shared my story, starting with the most recent events and going backward. He patiently listened and asked clarifying questions.

I have no doubt my stories were salacious enough for any lawyer to jump at the opportunity to represent me and take on the State Government Machine that had allowed me to fall through the cracks. But I'm glad I called Mike for advice and support. During the second hour of our initial meeting, he answered my questions and led me through my options moving forward. I wanted to know how I could make the bad behavior stop, and he provided options. I could continue documenting everything and essentially ride it out, waiting see what would happen after the legislative session ended. Perhaps my bosses would treat me differently when they were under less pressure. Another option was to file a complaint with the Iowa Civil Rights Commission and report what was going on while I continued to work in the environment.

The latter option scared me. I knew it was a tough one and it would probably make my situation worse.

I settled somewhere in the middle and decided to write a formal memo to my boss. I had previously verbalized my complaints three times, and no one had bothered to follow-up in written form or otherwise, so I knew it would take more than forceful words. I wanted documentation of my grievances and a pathway to change in my office.

I worked on a rough draft in Mike's office and took it home to flesh out. I told Mike I would submit the memo the very next morning and let him know what the response was.

After a break to have dinner with my family, I returned to work, refining the memo. I poured over it for hours, well past my bedtime and until my eyes could barely stay open. I saved, printed, and signed the document. On Friday, I arrived at my cubicle a few minutes after 8:00 a.m., ready to deliver it to my staff director.

The memo made several critical points:

- In five years as Communications Director, I always had good performance reviews and received no complaints about my work.

- Then suddenly, after I reported concerns about the work environment, I was informed that my work was unsatisfactory. My work efforts were subjected to intense criticism and micromanagement.

- Additionally, repeated requests to be included in key meetings—meetings that would inform my work—were denied.

- Given the abrupt change in attitude, I could only conclude that my recent complaints about the boys' club atmosphere in the office, the failure to adopt meaningful sexual harassment policies, and the continuously crude and hostile office work environment had touched a nerve.

In the memo, I requested a thorough investigation into the sexually hostile work environment, and at the same time, as a demonstration of my good will, I offered to assist the implementation of change in whatever way I could.

After I turned in my memo, I had trouble focusing on my work. Nothing remarkable occurred until just after 3:00 p.m. when the staff director came into the cubicle area.

"Alright everyone, it's Friday afternoon. Get a jump on the weekend. Finish what you're doing and head out of here," he said. Then he looked at me, stepped closer and lowered his voice. "Except you, Kirsten. I need you to stick around and meet me in the conference room in half an hour."

"Oh, okay," I said. The staff director returned to his office. I immediately looked at Jan, the only other woman in the office and my closest confidant. Jan knew that I had submitted the memo earlier in the morning.

After hastily collecting her things, she scurried to my cubicle, "Are you okay?"

"Yeah. Maybe he finally wants to talk about my memo." I said nervously.

"Sure." She gave me a sad and conciliatory look, which heightened my nervousness. "Just be strong and call me as soon as your meeting is over."

I grabbed my phone and stepped into the women's restroom to call Mike. I told him that everyone left the office, but I had to stay and was unsure why. "Maybe the memo will finally make change happen," I said.

"Maybe," Mike replied.

"What else should I say?"

"Just continue to ask about helping update the policies and procedures. And remember, you're in the right to ask for updated policies and to ask for the harassment and retaliation to stop. Don't worry too much about this meeting. Call me as soon as it's over."

I remember thinking optimistically that I was finally being heard and taken seriously.

I entered the conference room to find the senate minority leader—the top boss—already seated at the long conference room table, awaiting my arrival. Silently, he rested his elbows on the table, fingers clasped together. The staff director sat next to him and gestured for me to sit across from them. It created an intimidating triangle; two of them, one of me.

I physically stiffened as the staff director began to speak. "We have authority from the majority leader to terminate your employment immediately. If you choose to resign instead, we'll give you a recommendation," he said.

His words were a punch to the gut. My mind raced as I struggled to comprehend them. He was suddenly telling me he would write me a *recommendation*? He would recommend me and my work for some other job? Work that he continually picked apart and made me cry over? How could work that he deemed so poor suddenly be fine enough for a recommendation to someone else?

"I will not resign," I said.

"Okay. Turn in your badge, give me the YouTube password, and delete your legislative e-mail account from your phone before you leave the building." As he spoke, the senate minority leader remained silent, his fingers entwined on top of the conference room table. The conversation was over.

As I left the room, fury pulsated through my veins. I looked back over my shoulder, directly at the minority leader. "You'll be hearing from my attorney."

I collected the belongings from my desk, put them into a box that had suddenly appeared, and broke down in tears.

THE POWER OF DECISION

The decision to submit that memo of complaint on May 17, 2013 changed my life in more ways than I can count. It set me on a journey that led to serious soul searching. It also prompted me to go out into the world and make change the best way I know how: through education. Although the issue of workplace harassment ripples through families and communities across this country, it's rarely discussed. That needs to change. If we want to live and work in spaces and places free from sexual harassment, bullying, and retaliation, we must discuss it; good, bad and ugly.

That's what this book is all about, the good, bad, and ugly, because it matters. It matters to people you might not expect. Like your grandmother, who experienced inappropriate behavior and never said anything because it was "just so long ago." It matters to your best friend who was the butt of a sexual joke and did not know how to respond as everyone else laughed. It matters to kids who sense stress and anxiety in parents and then try and hide their own pain. These painful feelings don't necessarily go away. Many times, they're buried as a coping mechanism. They burrow under our skin as guilt or shame and gnaw at our sense of self-worth.

We must resurrect these feelings and deal with them. Our reactions to others' pain and to our own, and how we handle them matter. I'm living proof that bad situations can change, reactions can evolve, and we can bounce back from bad things with help and support. We can make amazing lemonade from pretty screwed up lemons, but first we must make the decision to start squeezing.

The average adult makes thirty-five thousand decisions a day of different weights and consequences. They range from what to wear and eat or which route to take to work to whether or not a divorce is the solution to marital problems. Decision-making can overwhelm some people, so much so that an entire industry is built upon reducing the burden and number of decisions in an effort to free up brain space for other things. Those "solutions" might be great for some, but to me it's sheer laziness to fill the closet with black turtlenecks to avoid having to choose clothes and clear up a tiny amount of head space for another menial task. The decisions we face daily are, most often, inconsequential in themselves. It is our response to them that define us. My decision to sue my employer was easy. I was desperate and at an all-time mental low point in my life. When you're desperate, it changes your viewpoint. I had nothing left to lose and nowhere to go but up!

I think about decisions on a sliding scale. For example, my decision to have a child rated a hard ten in difficulty. The decision was something my husband and I discussed at length. We weighed the pros and cons of bringing another life into this world. We discussed far-fetched scenarios, both positive and negative, regarding a baby. We talked about the child's health and wellbeing as well as how we would respond to certain situations if they arose. We wanted to take an honest approach to parenthood and be fully prepared for anything.

My decision to sue my employer was not even close to ten in difficulty, despite what you might think. When I weighed pros and cons— and the cons far outweighed the pros— I found myself at a point where I had nothing left to lose, a point of desperation. Making decisions from a low and desperate place essentially eased the burden for me. The only way forward was up the mountain since I was already living in the cave below it.

I knew I wasn't the same person I had been on February 1, 2008, my first day on the job in the Iowa Senate. That woman was full of optimism, excitement, and a desire to prove herself through exemplary writing and a tenacious work ethic. By the time I was fired in 2013, I was a timid, angry, jealous, and fearful person who cried at the drop of a hat and worried about what people thought of her.

Harassment is a game of power and control, and it had taken mine away. I longed to feel worthy, and that reduced me to an annoying people-pleaser. I reasoned that if people liked me, it would be harder for them to say and do mean things to me. I was so far away from the bright and happy woman I had been in 2008 that it made me angry. I had nothing to left to lose by 2013, and that made my decision easier.

That doesn't mean I didn't care about the outcome of my decision. I wanted to mitigate the risk for my coworkers. They made a choice not to come forward with me and instead stay where they were. I didn't want to see them fired too. I cared less about me because I had nowhere left to go but up. When you are pushed down so low that you think very little of yourself, your decisions all seem unimportant. This is what depression and anxiety do to a person. They are the dark weights hanging like a yoke around your neck, impacting everything you say and do.

THE AFTERMATH

Getting out of bed was hard, especially after I was fired, but knowing that I would have my time in court helped me rise daily. I needed to bring in an income for my family so that got me out of bed too. I spent time online looking for work and applying for jobs. Journaling helped tremendously (I highly recommend it). I wrote letters to my aggressors detailing my feelings and outlining my anger, letters they will never see. I wrote alternative scenarios for my situation. In those empowering fantasies, I made protestations for the harassment to stop, and my boss swooped in after hearing the egregious remarks. He backed me up and reprimanded Al for making disgusting comments that were so unfit for even the roughest of personalities to handle. In another scenario, I was appointed as chair of a committee tasked to update policies and procedures.

Playing out happy endings in my mind helped. Slowly, I came to know myself again because I was free from the toxicity. I surrounded myself with the friends and family I had neglected when long and tough work hours had consumed me. It was a long climb up that mountain from the cave.

Many people are climbing that mountain right now. When contemplating tough decisions, it's important to remember the emotional factor. Emotions drive responses and decisions. I'm a highly emotional person who wears my feelings on my sleeve. I used to be embarrassed by this fact but now I embrace it. Vulnerability is powerful, no matter what you have previously been told. I like to give and receive hugs—always with permission—and I'm not afraid to deny hugs if I'm mad at you. Just ask my family; that's how they know we need to have a discussion.

Recognizing the emotional response that a potential decision elicits within you is important. It can change your decision trajectory. Does thinking about that work project outcome make you anxious, queasy? Why? The answers might help you make your decisions. I've learned how to avoid letting my emotions get the better of me. I take a breath and slow down to identify the emotion being elicited. Then I ask some challenging questions: Why am I feeling this way? Is there a deeper cause or issue going on that is making me feel this way? Is the issue good or bad? Does my decision need to reflect that?

THINK ABOUT IT

- Don't let your emotions hijack your life and especially your decision-making. Some of this comes back to a choice in reaction; how we choose to do things and how we view the outcomes.

- Embrace and examine your emotional journey rather than fight or ignore it. Recognize that your emotions can be guideposts.

- How are decisions impacting your life? Are you facing decision fatigue? What are the emotions that bubble up around your decisions?

- How you handle tough decisions will define you and your outcomes.

PUT IT TO WORK: AMBER ENDURES THE PUB

Amber is a college town bartender who mixes amazing drinks from anything in a liquor cabinet. With just over a decade of experience, she enjoys helping customers find new beverages they never thought they would like. She built up a fanbase over the years and enjoys interacting with returning patrons.

Her bartending career began when she was a struggling student who needed money for college expenses. When she had a baby, everything changed. She had to drop out of school and return to bartending as a full-time career to support her child.

Whenever she can, Amber picks up extra shifts behind the bar or helps as a waitress. She used to play into the flirtatious banter some pub patrons would throw her way, hoping to get larger tips, but over the years, the banter has become an annoyance. Amber loathes it even though she knows it impacts the income she so desperately needs.

About a year or so ago, the bar owner hired a new manager, Ralph, who became Amber's boss. From the start, his attention set off alarm signals. He touches Amber at every opportunity and eyes her up and down with a gaze that makes her uneasy. One afternoon, he gropes her breast. Amber slaps his hands away.

Ralph grins and tells her that even though she's used to things going a certain way around the pub, times are changing. His expression hardens as he continues to reinforce the fact that he's the new boss and that she needs to work a little harder.

Amber replies by stating she already works very hard.

Ralph leans back, motions to his crotch and tells her that working hard is now a pay-to-play situation if she wants to keep working her current shifts.

Amber's stomach heaves in disgust. She storms out of his office, marches down the street, and applies at the pub that had, for years, competed with her old employer. Her reputation as an excellent bar tender is well known, and she is offered a new job immediately.

While Amber works hard to establish herself as a valued employee at the new bar, her reputation comes under attack from the old one. Ralph is spreading rumors out of spite. It's a small town, and people gossip. Things must go well with her new job. The town is big enough to offer some opportunities for employment, but small enough that the bar scene is fiercely competitive. If she loses this job, the rumors Ralph started may prevent her from finding another one.

While Amber works hard to establish herself as a valued employee at the new bar, her reputation comes under attack from the old one. Ralph is spreading rumors out of spite. It's a small town, and people gossip. Things have to go well with her new job. The town is big enough to offer some opportunities for employment, but small enough that the bar scene is fiercely competitive. If she loses this job, the rumors Ralph started may prevent her from finding another one.

The patron approaches Amber in the alley, furious. He is even more intoxicated than he was when Amber refused to serve him. He grabs her and attempts to push her down. Amber fights back. Amid the tussle, she suffers some bruises and scrapes but she's able to push the inebriated man to the ground and escape.

Thoroughly shaken, Amber doesn't want to report the incident. She certainly doesn't want to tell the pub manager what happened. Because of the gossip fueled by her old boss, she is afraid she'll be blamed for the attack. She is also terrified about what will happen when her assailant returns to the pub for a drink.

ASSESS THE SITUATION

- What are all the issues at play in this situation?

- What emotions are driving Amber's decision making?

- Is there a "right thing" for Amber to do?

- Should she say something to her manager? The police? The patron?

- What alternative reactions could Amber have chosen in these circumstances of harassment and abuse?

- How can Amber proactively protect herself?

- What can Amber do to feel safer at work?

CHAPTER 3
THE WHEELS OF JUSTICE

Legal action can be financially draining. The complexity of the process can take a toll on a family and on the plaintiff's mental and physical well-being.

AFTER BEING TERMINATED, I was faced with a huge reality check and a long learning journey. Because I knew my case was justified, I thought it would be open-and-shut. What I considered to be a clear abuse of power by lawmakers burst onto the Iowa scene quickly and brightly. Then reality set in. The search for justice was reduced to a slow burn and four-year legal battle. My experience was nothing close to a television drama where the crime, trial prep, and jury verdict happen within one sixty-minute episode. Fortunately, my lawyer, Mike, quickly dispelled the legal myths I had floating in my head and deftly leveled my expectations—including the naïve notion that my harasser would suddenly feel remorse and voluntarily apologize.

Yeah, that never happens.

I'm forever grateful that my lawyer always told me what I needed to hear rather than what I wanted to hear. Needs and wants have wildly conflicting aspects on the reality spectrum, and a person can go down a rabbit hole of negativity if they aren't properly tempered.

PREPARING FOR COURT

In my initial conversations with Mike, I made it clear that I wanted several outcomes from the case:

1. a public apology from the person who fired me—the senate minority leader;

2. for the harasser and those who retaliated against me to lose their jobs;

3. for policies to change, allowing a better reporting process, and ultimately, a better working environment; and

4. fair compensation for lost employment, career interruption, and lost earning potential.

I was naïve going into the legal process. Mike immediately warned me that my first and second demands would never be met. He was right. You cannot mandate an apology or job termination through the civil litigation process. Over time, I tempered my wants with my needs. The last two items on my wish list were more reasonable and worth fighting for.

Mike and his two colleagues, who comprised my legal team, were patient with me. To gain a thorough understanding of operating procedures, as is my tendency, I asked a lot of questions and posed plenty of potentially unrealistic scenarios to them. They responded thoughtfully and pleasantly to every single one. Every step of the way, my lawyers treated me as a partner in a daunting and scary legal battle. They never talked down to me and always consulted me before making any decisions. I had a true voice in how my legal case unfolded, from which steps were taken and not taken to selecting the most beneficial lines of questioning. I now understand that successful legal cases are always fought and won through partnerships.

Mike always pushed me, but never so far that his requests encroached upon my limits. If he was unsure about boundary lines, he asked. He pressed me to attend as many depositions as I could, even though we both knew how uncomfortable it would make me. I had to face people who fired me, spoke ill of me, made fun of me, and thought poorly of me. I had to listen to opinions of me and my work as though I weren't sitting in the same room.

With each deposition I attended—about a dozen in total—my strength grew and my skin thickened. Mike showed me how he used psychology as a tool to help with questioning. Several men who were deposed clearly struggled with his approach; they sweated and stammered when he questioned them. A few of them looked disheveled, which was a stark contrast to the crisp suits and confident, nonchalant attitudes I experienced at the state capitol.

In person, seated with our lawyers at the same table and unable to avoid me, my opposers seemed small. That made me feel good. A few times, Mike paused depositions after asking an important question, simply to build tension. We'd step out of the little conference room, go to another side of the office, confer about what just happened, wait a bit, and relax. Those breaks turned the tables. It squeezed the person being deposed and gave them a taste of what it felt like to face uncomfortable questions. That helped me feel better.

We partnered throughout the entire legal process, which was a series of two steps forward, one step back. Technicalities, appeals, gathering information, and waiting for responses and for a trial date extended my legal quest into a four-year battle. I won my case in July of 2017. Just a few months later in the fall, Al Schuster, the longtime staffer who harassed me and my other colleagues, left. Whether he left on his own or was forced to resign, I don't know, but he was gone.

When the senate minority leader left office not long after Al Schuster went, his handpicked staff director and Chief Advisor Goldman—the two bosses who had retaliated against me—went with him. I got a sense from the trial process and interacting with these men that they felt no remorse. They never truly understood the pain and mental anguish they caused me. I'm not optimistic they will ever understand the harm done or the ripple effect it created both inside and outside the office.

ON TRIAL

After I was fired, I switched careers knowing I would never return to political communications. I found a job as a fundraising professional. When my trial began in April of 2017, I left that fundraising job to throw myself into the legal process. I attended all the depositions of my former coworkers and legislators I could. Going into the summer of 2017, I strategized daily with my legal team. I spent hours at their office combing through the eleven thousand emails that were submitted as evidence. We spent hour after hour rehearsing questions—not only what *should* be asked, but what *would* be asked of me—and my responses. The legal battle was my full-time job for several months. I was so consumed with ensuring my side of the story would be effectively heard by a jury that I don't remember much else from that period. It was exhausting.

I'm eternally grateful to my husband and son for picking up the pieces around me. They carried on and were extremely supportive. They extended grace when I missed family dinners or forgot appointments or neglected to pack my son's lunch for the day. My husband just did it without me. He was a single parent for a time, and I'm forever grateful and appreciative of him and his efforts.

Legal action should be a last resort for any target. If a person is not mentally strong enough or doesn't have a support system to tap into, or thick, alligator-like skin and the ability to be patient, they should not entertain the idea of legal recourse. Legal action can be financially draining. The complexity of the legal process can take a toll on a family and on the plaintiff's mental and physical well-being.

Although the system may seem frustrating with all its procedural steps and time delays, it's not entirely a bad thing. Its checks and balances were put in place by our forefathers to ensure a free and fair system. Citizens have a right to their day in court. Many decisions rest on the shoulders of a fair and unbiased representation of our society—juries comprised of societal peers. Thanks to the assistance of my lawyers, I was able to easily navigate the system.

FINDING LEGAL REPRESENTATION

From what I've briefly relayed about my experience, you can see the important role my lawyers played. If you decide to look for a lawyer, ask a lot of questions. What approach will the lawyer take to pursue your case? Will the lawyer want to work with you on a contingency fee basis (a fee paid only if a case is won) or on retainer (a fee paid in advance to secure services)? Know the difference between the two and how it can affect your pocketbook in the short and long-term.

Before we started working together, Mike walked me through the payment process and the difference between working on a retainer or a contingency basis. He pointed out important items in our contract as they came up. Nothing was hidden from me. I was treated as an equal. These may seem like small matters in the whole scheme of things, but to a person who is already struggling, providing information and support with such clarity is important. For me, it created a semblance of sanity during a nerve-wracking process. Having a strong, confident, and empathetic lawyers like Mike and his partners fighting my legal battle certainly made a difference for me. It helped me achieve the sense of triumph, relief, and even validation that were instrumental in my positive outcome.

THINK ABOUT IT

- Legal battles can be long and laborious, taking a significant toll on finances, relationships, and mental health.

- Choosing to go to court—or not—should be well thought out.

- Make sure your lawyer is willing to answer your questions and thoroughly prepare you for each step along the way.

- Remember that who you choose as your lawyer and how they are willing to work with you impacts the proceedings and the results.

PUT IT TO WORK: MARTA AND THE MOTEL

Marta is a 45-year-old immigrant who works on the cleaning crew at a local motel. She came to the US full of optimism and enthusiasm for the American Dream. She is now married with children and has a steady, decent-paying job in a community that largely does not know she is here illegally.

Her job at the motel is consistent. Her boss is kind and accommodating, especially when it comes to her children. He is willing to move her shifts around when she encounters family emergencies or childcare issues. For the most part, Marta enjoys her work and her coworkers, who hail from all over the globe. Like Marta, some of them are in the US illegally. As a result, the cleaning crew is close. They confide in each other about the challenges of their jobs, including difficulty dealing with motel patrons. Harassment and sexual aggression aren't unusual.

One evening, Marta is propositioned by a female guest to join in on "some fun" that is clearly sexual in nature. When Marta refuses, the female motel patron grows hostile. She makes a formal complaint about Marta, her service, and her skills. Although the complaint is clearly unwarranted and Marta has the support of her boss, it's noted in her record in compliance with the motel's processes and procedures. Marta doesn't need another complaint as she fears it may cost her this job.

And then another incident shakes Marta to the core.

She knocks on the door of a motel room and announces her arrival as housekeeping staff. She waits a moment and then knocks again. When there is no response, she uses her key, props the door open with its door stop, and enters the room with her cleaning cart. The room is dark and quiet, the bed a mound of twisted covers. She turns away from the bed to turn on the lights. Suddenly, a pair of hands grab her buttocks. Marta screams and tries to twist away. When she manages to turn around, she faces a naked man. She screams again. He puts his finger over his lips, motioning her to be silent.

Marta wrenches away. The naked man pleads with her to stay, be quiet, enjoy what's to come. He grabs Marta's shoulder, shoves her against the wall and rips off her blouse. Marta manages to wrestle away and escape the room through the propped-open door, leaving her cleaning cart and blouse behind. She goes straight to the motel laundry room where she hopes to find another coworker, but the room is empty.

Marta needs help, but she's too scared to move, let alone speak. How does she explain what happened? What should she do now? How can she get her cart and her clothing back? So many questions!

As upset as Marta is, she knows it is not worth filing paperwork over the incident and risk losing her job or being exposed as an illegal immigrant. She does not want law enforcement involved in the situation for the same reason. It is also not worth angering her spouse who already worries about her daily. She feels she has nowhere to turn.

All Marta wants to do is help provide for her family, ensure her children live better than she did, and give them a fighting chance for their future.

ASSESS THE SITUATION

- What is Marta's best course of action after the incident?

- How can Marta get the support she needs?

- Does being fair or right matter in this situation?

- Are there ways Marta can let go of her fears to pursue justice?

- Does this situation affect more than just Marta?

- What are some policies or procedures that could be put in place to better protect workers like Marta?

CHAPTER 4
LIFE BEFORE AND AFTER

> What I went through was tough and at times, dark and lonely. It has made me who I am now.

THERE IS A "before" and an "after" in my life. Everything career-related that happened to me before and during my time at the Iowa Statehouse is my "before" life, and everything that followed my firing is my "after" life.

I don't see myself as remarkable in any way, nor am I exceptional in my thinking or frame of mind. My "before" life is standard, average, and I dare say, boring. Like so many others, I worked hard to advance my career. I took on challenges that would bring positive experiences and help me grow in the process. I had the same goals, dreams, and desires that most professionals share: to garner a semblance of success, contribute to society in a positive way, and make a decent living.

These goals and dreams were stunted and forever changed upon the termination of my employment with the Iowa Legislature as Communications Director. My future earning was compromised, my career trajectory altered. How I came to be fired wasn't unique. Unfortunately, the terrible conditions I endured are still common. My reaction to what I endured—my choice to take a stand and speak up—was what made my circumstances stand out.

BEFORE

At daily caucus meetings, Senators discussed everything from legislation and how they would vote on important bills to the political events they would or would not attend. Inevitably, personal opinions spilled into the conversation. Many off-color jokes, disgusting comments, and inappropriate, unrelated chatter occurred. All staff were expected to attend. We had to endure the entire proceeding so we could answer any questions that arose.

Caucus was always a mixed bag for staff. We never knew what we were walking into. Once, a senator led a discussion on the act of tea-bagging. He tried to enlighten listeners about this potentially violent act which is sexual in nature. Another time, during a right-to-life discussion, a senator thought it appropriate to tell jokes about killing abortion doctors. I was surprised by all the laughs he garnered.

Many days were long. My job necessitated staying in the building till the very last vote was taken. I had to be available in case one of my bosses managed to get an amendment passed or wanted to make sure their home district knew how staunchly they opposed some piece of politically volatile legislation. Sometimes the legislation itself was less important than the vote cast or the action taken by the senator. I had to issue a press release to state and local media sharing their version of the story as quickly as possible. Being first to the media was often more important than being right, regardless of the time of day.

One evening, the minority senators held things up until the wee hours to stick it to the Governor over a nominee they didn't like. They ordered pizza and carried on jovially without bothering to discuss the merits, skills, and experience of the nominee, or the fact that there were no palatable alternatives. This display of petty annoyance was how the minority chose to operate at the time. It was the only true power they had, and they were exercising that power. Ultimately, the nominee was pulled from the slate and victory was claimed by those I worked for. This tactic of deflect and delay was a power muscle flexed often, and staff were not allowed to ask questions. Loyalty was demanded. That meant blindly following and taking orders. As you may guess, it was a recipe for disaster.

In addition to that ongoing pressure, minority leadership changed frequently, leading to a roller coaster of tension, let-down, and unanswered questions from staff. It was always clear that staff was relegated to the background. Our senators were not shy about putting us or our work down in front of others, if only to prove that we were subservient.

That point was proven one evening in 2013, when a senator summoned one of my coworkers. That particular senator had a notorious reputation for calling staff names and telling lewd jokes to intimidate others, so I decided to accompany my coworker to the senate floor for moral support.

"Did you file that bill I asked you about earlier in the day?" the senator asked.

"Yes. And I'm waiting on the fiscal note for it. I can go over the estimates with you right now if you want," my coworker offered politely.

"No!" the senator snarled. "I don't care about that. I didn't ask you for that."

"OK. Just let me know if you want to go over the numbers," my coworker replied calmly.

"No! Jeez, you're stupid! You don't listen! Did you not hear what I said? Stop being so stupid!" the senator roared angrily.

The conversation quickly turned into a Jekyll and Hyde moment of disbelief. The senator continued to thunder and called my coworker "stupid" a few more times. His message was clear: *regardless of what is done or said, I have power and control over you, and you will accept whatever I dish out.*

Stunned by the quick turn of events, we tried to extract ourselves from the situation as quickly as possible. Why would anyone act this way, unprovoked, and be so nasty to someone trying to help? The senator was nothing more than a bully.

Frequent leadership changes created disturbances among staff. Whenever roles shifted, we'd gather in our cubicle area to speculate about what lay ahead. While conjecture and rumor mills contributed to the already toxic atmosphere, they also provided an outlet for our fears, including the biggest one: *would we be terminated by new leadership?* Looking back, perhaps it was an omen. At the time, it seemed laughable.

During the five years I was employed by the Iowa government, I worked for four different minority leaders, three different chief legislative advisors, and three different staff directors. Each one had a different style, demeanor, and set of priorities. For the most part, they kept information close to the vest and were not open or honest about much of anything. This small and petty behavior hurt staff morale and instilled distrust amongst us. It also helped perpetuate fear—fear of retribution, fear of asking questions, and fear of change.

Honesty is always the best policy. Good leaders care about staff, their productivity, and the state of the workplace. They work to build trust rather than tear it down. Working for bosses who fell short of honesty was challenging.

The shortfalls of our bosses were made clear when I first complained about Al calling women derogatory names in the office. That was in 2010, with my co-worker, Jan, by my side. The staff director must have taken some form of action because Al was quiet for about a week. When his tirades picked up again, my response to him, regardless of tone or tact, did not seem to matter. There was zero accountability, zero consequences.

An aggressor or harasser can be good at their job and liked on a personal level and still be a jerk—and that is where the water gets murky. Al and I socialized.

I was asked more than once why I spent time with Al outside the office.

"Were you friends with Al?" asked one of the state's attorneys when I was on the witness stand.

"Yes."

"Did you have lunch with him?"

"Sure. Yes."

"Coffee?"

"Maybe. We might have walked to get coffee, yes."

"Drinks after work?"

"Yes." As I started to understand the direction of the questions, I bristled. They were attempting to make me look untrustworthy because I chose to spend free time with him. If I were reliable, how could I choose to spend time with someone who made my work life hard, embarrassing, and shameful?

"How often would that occur, those types of things, lunch, coffee, drinks after work?" the attorney continued.

"Maybe once a month."

"Did you ever have him over to your house or vice versa?"

"Yes." As I spoke the truth, shame and embarrassment crept in again. Jeff and I had invited Al over for dinner when he was struggling through his divorce, something we couldn't comprehend. Despite the fact that his office behavior was disturbing, I believed—and still believe—that everyone deserves kindness, especially when they are at a low point. But that didn't mean I had to accept his disgusting behavior in the office.

The state's attorney continued grilling me, drawing out details that made it look as though Al and I were close. Al helped us pick up furniture when we moved. He bought a birthday present for our son.

"So you would describe him as a friend?" the attorney asked.

"Yes." I said reluctantly as my stomach clenched. Any larger social interactions outside the office with Al were always tempered. The rants against women and dirty jokes didn't happen in front of my husband. During social gatherings at the bar after work with only staff present, Al's pompous, egotistical brags would continue, but it was never as loud or lewd. Maybe he tempered his attitude because we were in a public place with other eyes watching. I will never know. The office was clearly a space where he felt not only comfortable but powerful.

I never heard from Al or saw him after the day I was fired. He lived nearby, and for about two years, I had an irrational fear that I would run into him at a local store. I put off going to this store with my husband for a long time. When he finally confronted me about it, I came clean and told him about my fear of running into this man who made me feel small and worthless. I was nervous that Al would direct anger at me for being fired and dragging *his* name into the mud!

Jeff quickly told me to get over myself. He was right for a few reasons. First of all, I don't have the power and clout to hold sway over anything, especially someone else's anger. Second, I was the one who was fired and out of a job with a damaged reputation; Al still had the same job even though he was a harasser. I had misguided feelings of guilt, as if my situation was my own fault!

Third, and most importantly, my husband was with me and always would be, on several levels. It did not matter if we were confronted by anyone in public because he would be there. He reminded me that I had to stop living in fear.

People who are continually beaten down often have irrational thoughts related to fear:

How did I cause this?

What did I do to deserve this?

How do I respond?

How will I embarrass myself? Will I break down and cry?

How can I simply keep my head down today?

What will set my aggressor off today?

What will make me the target today?

All fearful thoughts. All valid. Notice these questions insinuate the target is the problem.

The moment my husband reassured me that he stood by me physically and mentally, my fears began to melt away. I needed a champion in my corner to let go of the fear. The fear took time to dissipate. Since that initial reassurance, many encouraging conversations have taken place between me and my champion husband. I need reminders that I have no reason to fear, that I am a strong, thoughtful, valued woman who is making a difference in the world. It's not as if a switch was thrown and I suddenly became fearless in every aspect of my life. NO. I battle my demons and struggle with low self-confidence. The difference is that I now recognize when I need reassurance and when I need to surround myself with friends and family for strength to help me be more fearless.

What I went through was tough and at times, dark and lonely. It has made me who I am now. It has helped me create deeper, more meaningful connections to others, including a mentor. This may seem like a small thing, however, I stubbornly and misguidedly thought I didn't need a mentor's support because I had the ability to figure things out on my own. Asking for help has never been my strong suit. My experiences with workplace harassment humbled me. They helped me realize that no one is an island in this world, and they shouldn't have to be. As humans, we thrive on connectivity. We are simply better together.

AFTER

People don't talk much about the "after" life or the fallout surrounding highly publicized sexual harassment cases. When Dr. Christine Bla-sey-Ford came forward and testified in front of the United States Senate Judiciary Committee in 2018, the public saw many things, among them the stress that a person exhibits in emotional, highly charged situations. Dr. Blasey-Ford's testimony about being sexually assaulted by a United States Supreme Court nominee thrust her into an unwanted spotlight. Not only that, the assault she experienced years earlier had altered her life and her thought-process moving forward—*her* "after" life. In her testimony, she stated that she had become the target of aggressive ha-rassment and even death threats, forcing her and her family to leave their home for an undisclosed location. She also testified that, due to fear from her assault years ago, she was more sensitive toward safety issues. In fact, she and her family designed their home to guard against intruders—with a multiple door entryway, for example. The traumatic experience appeared to drive her decision-making from the day of her assault forward.

People who have been thrust into the spotlight, especially through the legal system, can have their lives torn apart. It's as though the expo-sure puts their character on trial and gives the general public the right to invade whatever privacy might remain. When you're dealing with politicians, as I was, the problem is only made worse. Politicians pride themselves on the façade they present to their constituency. Even small-er-scale situations like mine threaten their public persona—and any threat to their image can be devastating, even if it comes from a seem-ingly insignificant woman like me. That's why they will go to extremes to protect it.

Because my case made headline news as far away as Great Britain and as close as next door, I was recognized every time I went out. While I didn't read the comments section of publicized stories, I was informed that the trolls were out in full force. One day, Jeff slammed down his phone after reading news coverage of my case. "Well, I think it's time we get a dog."

"Why?" I asked, surprised. We're a cat family. "Dogs are a lot of work."

"Because someone just made a bold comment on the latest Des Moines Register story about you and your case."

"What was it?" I asked.

"They said, 'Yeah, I'd harass her, too.' If that's the sentiment and you continue to do interviews and be outspoken, and continue to jog through the neighborhood alone, we need to think about protecting our family. A dog can help with that."

We eventually found our pup at the local animal shelter. Soldier—a name his previous owner gave him that fit him well—has personality to spare and a bark worse than his bite. He serves as a perfect protector for our family.

The emboldened mindset of online anonymity coupled with political spin created a recipe of tension and worry. "I'd harass her, too," was on the mild side. At other extreme were comments that I was crying wolf, trying to bring the political party down, or attempting to ruin politicians. People were upset. And when people become upset, they sometimes disregard logic. I needed to start thinking about how to respond to those types of reactions.

The after-effects of a life-changing situation are far-reaching. My husband and I had lengthy discussions that we never anticipated. We established rules or guidelines that our family would abide by to maintain some semblance of privacy. Because I refused to read the comments section in the major and local media outlets that ran stories on me and my trial, my long-time best friend patrolled them for me. She never reported anything out of the ordinary. I'm sure she wanted to keep the mean and nasty posts away by telling me it was all "status quo." I don't think anyone has threatened me or my family at this time. I hope it stays that way.

THE IMPACT ON OTHERS

Others have been affected by my decision to come forward, to speak up and do the right thing by holding my employer accountable. Aside from my family, my former coworkers probably felt the harshest aftermath of my termination. I'm not sure how my abrupt departure was explained to other staff, but it was undoubtedly awkward and potentially confusing for many.

Since I had spoken with a few of my coworkers right after being fired, they knew my side of things. They had experienced many similar situations in their own right. Explaining my termination beyond my coworkers was more complicated, especially after I went to the press with my story two days later. It was messy and felt as much. I spent a lot of time thinking, worrying, and praying for my coworkers in the tension-filled environment I left behind. It was hard to not talk to them and ask how they were doing or what was going on or how the office was handling my absence with all the communication-related items that take place at the end of a legislative session. I had a hard time comprehending how the work I'd done would continue without me. But it did, and it doesn't matter how it was taken care of. Everyone wants to feel indispensable, but there is no sugar-coating the fact that everyone is replaceable in their jobs. Computer files aren't tough to access. Lists and outline processes are easy to follow when in place. Most often, the person behind the computer is less important than the information shared.

My former coworkers had to pick up the slack, but they also had to deal with an aftermath of workplace harassment that is not often discussed: fear. They worried that they might be fired next should they speak out, and that the training mandated by the court would not be taken seriously, because leadership didn't recognize the toxicity, didn't want change, and didn't want to be held accountable to anyone.

New training did take place. From what I've heard, plenty of jokes about it are circulating through the office. That tells me the training wasn't taken seriously.

Another common concern arising from sexual harassment cases is fear of the pendulum swinging too far the other way—men going to extremes to avoid working with and talking to women in the office in case innocent behavior is misconstrued and reported as harassment. There is also the risk of the super-patronizing, sorry-not-sorry approach to the locker room banter that prefaces off-color jokes with, "Now, don't go reporting me, but have you heard this one...."

You can imagine the impact that this type of atmosphere can have on individuals as well as organizations. Damaged morale and a lack of leadership attention fosters distrust and resentment, causing productivity to plummet. Facing extreme situations at work is terrible for employees and does not allow anyone to succeed.

MOVING FORWARD

More changes are still needed to make the Iowa Statehouse a better, safer, more modern place to work, but statehouses aren't the only places that need updating. Workplaces everywhere must institute policies and procedures regarding sexual harassment. If policies and procedures are already in place, they must be updated, streamlined for uniformity, and enforced throughout departments. Multiple reporting chains are a must as well. If your workplace doesn't have a system in place, establish one now. It will help boost employee trust and confidence and in turn, its overall public image.

Finally, mandating training videos as the sole mechanism for employee education is outdated. There is typically no accountability tied to this approach. Even if employees are required to take a test after watching, they'll forget about what they learned until they are forced to repeat the process a year later. However, when organizational leaders follow up with open dialogue and even accountability measures, employees have no choice but to actively engage in the process.

To increase employee commitment to dealing with harassment in the workplace, I helped create an in-person training program. It works in tandem with *I Said Something,* a video I helped write and produce. Designed to shift the #MeToo movement into a movement of action, I'm happy to say that this training video is short in duration, drives home the point quickly, and it's backed up with thought-provoking questions that foster trust and build on team dialogue for understanding. The training centers around accountability and consequences when it comes to sexual harassment, bullying, and retaliation—something not often talked about.

Bottom line: the old videos with a white-haired man putting a hand on a female's back side while spouting inuendoes will prompt so much laughter that you and your team will not be able to focus on anything else. Conduct research to find comprehensive, impactful training. Do more than watch a video.

Remaining strong in light of my experience and speaking out about the multi-layered misery of workplace harassment has been interesting. My "after" life is far from boring. Traveling the country post-firing and speaking to groups of all ages has been an amazing opportunity for me. Because there aren't many women out there who sue a state, win, and go on to discuss lessons learned, doors have opened to me. I've had the privilege of meeting wonderful people, and I relish the opportunity to discuss with them the lessons I've learned. Because people are willing to engage in that discussion, it means they still care.

We learn the most from our failures. Thomas Edison once said: "I have not failed. I've just found ten thousand ways that won't work." I love this quote because it has so many lessons wrapped up in two sentences. Resiliency, bravery, and confidence emerge when you can admit so many "wrongs" were required to ensure the "right" came along.

Tackling the heavy and complex issue of workplace harassment requires resiliency, bravery, and confidence. Every time I talk to an audience, group, or individual, I point to those traits. What happened to me was awful and wrong. It required bravery and confidence to stand up for what's right. I'm stronger and better for doing so, more resilient.

I hope each person is able to utilize their personal strengths in their own situations regardless of stature, class, or title. One of the greatest lessons I learned from going through this experience is the fact that I could handle more than I thought I could. The same goes for everyone else: You *can* handle more than you think you can.

THINK ABOUT IT

- Don't let fearful thoughts overpower your life. Try to discern if your fears are rational or irrational.

- Pause and consider what you truly have control over and what that means for your situation.

- Don't just watch a training video to alleviate toxicity in your workplace. There is so much more that can and should be done to make work environments safer and more engaging. Initiating a conversation with co-workers and organizational leaders is a good place to start—ask about the policies and procedures currently in place.

- We learn from failure and resiliency; bravery and confidence help get us there.

- You can handle more than you think you can.

PUT IT TO WORK:
LORRAINE LOOKS ON

Lorraine has been around her workplace for a long time. Over the years, she took on many different jobs with increasing responsibility. She gave each role her all to help grow the company. After years of hard work, she is finally in a position to make decisions that will shape organizational direction. She is a leader who spends much of her professional time sharing industry knowledge and cranking out results for her company. She can proudly say she never threw anyone under the bus or compromised her values to get where she is.

Lorraine is now close to retirement. She has a few good years left and wants to leave while she's at the top of her game. It's time to start working on a succession plan. However, she's preoccupied by her new role as caregiver for her aging mother, whom she accompanies to numerous doctor appointments and recently moved into her own home. Lorraine is struggling to process her mother's recent Alzheimer's Disease diagnosis and her ongoing decline. Lorraine's bosses know about her situation, and they have been accommodating. They let her skip meetings or join them remotely, leave work early as necessary, and so on.

As Lorraine is busy focusing on her personal life, her former superior and now colleague, Don, has intensified his harassment of the young professionals in their office. Lorraine has witnessed many instances where Don shouts at them or makes inappropriate jokes and inuendoes. Don has never targeted or directed his aggressions at Lorraine. She's thankful for that. Don reacts vindictively to any form of confrontation or questions about how he gets things done. The last person who challenged him was demoted and sent to work at another company location.

Lately, Lorraine has noticed that everyone in the office seems to be avoiding Don. Although Lorraine is in a position to do something about Don's behavior, she is so busy and overwhelmed by her own life circumstances that she brushes difficult situations aside. With retirement and her mother on her mind, she has much more important things to think about.

ASSESS THE SITUATION

- How is Lorraine doing a disservice to the company by not saying anything to Don, the employees, or the company's human resources department (HR)?

- How can Lorraine be brave, resilient, and confident in her workplace despite her personal situation?

- What might Lorraine do to stand up for or with those around her while honoring her own challenges?

- Does a power dynamic come into play in this scenario? What is potentially at stake if Lorraine says nothing?

CHAPTER 5
STICKS AND STONES

> The more time you spend as the butt of someone else's jokes, being called derogatory names, or simply being picked on, the worse you feel in general, and the more you start to believe what you're hearing.

"STICKS AND STONES may break my bones, but words will never hurt me."

The familiar childhood rhyme is crap. No matter how hard you may try to let hurtful words bounce off, some words sting and sting hard. They may not leave a visible wound, rather a deep, gut-punch bruise that knocks you back and takes a bit to recover from.

Let's be honest, when people are in a verbally abusive relationship, their mental well-being is affected. A 2017 study showed that one in five American workers faced verbal abuse of some sort in the span of a month.[4] Being a verbal punching bag is extremely damaging to a person's psyche. It can affect everything they do, from choosing what clothes to wear to setting a route from the car to the desk.

As I approached my final breaking point, I was consumed by fear and uncertainty over what might happen at the office. Would I be the butt of a sex joke? Would my boss call me names that would make me cry? I forced myself to analyze negative possibilities and strategize how to mitigate potential risks so that I could maintain dignity and control. It was a losing battle, full of wild cards. I never knew who would be at the Capitol visiting a legislator or what issue might arise to throw me or my coworkers off our game, angering our bosses. I was mentally and emotionally exhausted.

The more time you spend as the butt of someone else's jokes, being called derogatory names, or simply being picked on, the worse you feel in general, and the more you start to believe what you're hearing. The more your self-confidence tanks. It's a feeling of helplessness and surrender that presses heavily against your chest; a weight you cannot push off. It's something only those who have been targets will grasp.

I liken my daily existence at the Capitol in 2013 to the plight of a boxer entering the ring daily to face a serious heavyweight matchup. Hard punches were sure to come, but whether I would get up from blow to blow was a crapshoot. Until the day I was fired, I managed to get back up each time, and thank goodness, I never received a TKO (total knockout).

Words hurt. It doesn't matter how thick your skin is or if you tell yourself to let them roll off your back: words meant to hurt actually *do* hurt. It's how long you *let* them hurt you that makes the difference.

Do you allow them to sting for a hot minute and let them go? Or do you allow them to occupy precious mental space and debilitate you for a week? Do you stew about them, overthink them, replay the verbal assault in your mind and ruminate about how it could, would, or should have turned out differently if only you had said or done something different?

Every single time I was the butt of someone's joke or called *dumb* or *bitch*—or worse, the *C* word—it stung. Some instances I protested, some I stewed over. Would I have felt better if I had protested more or said something funny to deflect the pain or even yelled a hurtful epithet back at my aggressor? The truth is that an equally aggressive and mean response would have just been mean and aggressive. It would have made me feel worse because that behavior is not me and never will be. Stooping to another level of mean or hurtful behavior is not natural for most people. That's a good thing. We need more kind, caring, empathetic individuals in this world!

Acknowledging that words hurt is a great step toward self-realization and self-confidence, or at least toward being real and honest with yourself. Choosing to let the sting last no longer than a minute will help you bounce back more easily than letting it sting for a week. And it is a choice, a difficult one, but still a choice. It also helps to remember that karma is real and will eventually visit people who are mean and say hurtful things.

I pity people who feel the need to bully others. They lack true happiness in their life.

THE GIFT OF GRACE

One more crucially important tip: give yourself more grace. Extend the same grace to yourself you would extend to someone else. Be as kind and forgiving and gentle with yourself as you would with someone else. It does not matter if you think you deserve it or not. You simply need to *do* it. Grace provides allowance for your humanness and makes more room in your life for the unknowns. It allows you to take the higher ground and let go of things a little quicker. Letting go is not about allowing hurtful words or stinging barbs to roll off your back. It's about acknowledging your emotions and thoughts, accepting them as legitimate, and taking the time you need to process them. That's grace. That's where learning and growth take place. That's where healing occurs.

Grace needs wiggle room to thrive. Lots of people talk about attaining perfection and believe its achievement will open doors or mean great things. They don't stop to give themselves room to assess the unknowns, the unanticipated circumstances. They don't stop to smell the roses because they're too focused on cultivating orchids. When they finally do catch the scent of a rose—possibly by accident—a whole new world opens. They suddenly realize the world is a garden of scents and take note of the beautifully perfumed hydrangeas, too.

I was able to get back up from the punches I received at my job because I gave myself grace. Grace allowed me to feel my pain and admit that I was hurt, that I wasn't some superhero immune to it all. I gave myself grace to feel angry, vengeful, mournful, even happy that it was happening to me and not someone who was unable to handle it. Although it hurt, I knew I was still a good person who deserved respect. I was stronger than most and I wanted to prove it.

After my high-profile trial and winning my case, many people came out of the woodwork wanting to talk to me. Some sought my advice, and some wanted to be attached to my name. I imagine some simply wanted to meet me and see what all the hype was about. I spent months with a fully booked calendar of coffee meetings and lunches with strangers.

I allowed this to happen because I felt it was important to take time with people who wanted to know me. If someone went to the trouble of contacting me, they clearly needed to get something off their chest and felt I was the one who should hear it. Often, they believed we had some sort of connection, which I appreciated immensely. However, being so available to others drained my spirit. In one instance, my coffee mate barely let me get a word in edgewise. Instead, they talked about themselves, their situation and what they wanted to do with their life. I relived my own trauma with every interaction. I had to step back and take more time for my family or risk letting the trauma continue to consume me. I was—and still am—personally compelled to help others because I feel strongly that no one should go through what I went through on their own, but I eventually learned to ask critical questions ahead of time. How did they think I could help them? What was their goal in meeting with me? I'm a patient listener, but I'm not a therapist. Many people I met with probably needed a trained professional.

Extensive giving of yourself and your time for others is exhausting. I have started using "No," "Not at this time," and "Here's a resource for you," instead of a blanket, "Yes." I now do a much better job screening people and meetings. I know how to get to the heart of their issues in order to see if I can truly help them or not. Know that you cannot be everything for everyone. Know that your time and energy are precious resources. Give yourself a bit of grace so that you can extend grace to others without depleting yourself.

DO SOMETHING

Bystander and upstander intervention can help ease the burden of sticks and stones and change lives in the process. That means stepping in and speaking out when inappropriate behavior is experienced or witnessed, regardless of your relationship with the aggressor and/or target. No one should have to take on a bully alone. There is strength in numbers. We are better together. No one should witness inappropriate behavior and look the other way.

I constantly remind those I meet that they have the power to turn #MeToo into #ISaidSomething. Stepping out and standing up builds trust and a sense of teamwork within an organization and eliminates siloed behavior and mentality.

All too often we witness or experience inappropriate situations and do nothing because it feels awkward. We need to get comfortable with necessary and appropriate interventions. Trust me, it takes practice. So practice verbalizing phrases that have been proven to work. Practice in the mirror, recognizing the non-verbal cues you project as you speak. Practice with a trusted friend or loved one so they know and understand what you are going through. It's good for you, and it's good for them.

Here are some phrases that are easily interchangeable in a variety of settings. They work. I've tested them.

- I don't find that funny.

- I heard some raised voices and just wanted to see if everything was okay.

- The joke/comment/email message you shared was not appropriate for a workplace environment.

- What you just said could be misinterpreted so please don't share it again.

- Those comments you made aren't appreciated by everyone in the office.

- Personal criticism should not be shared at the office.

- Please look me in the eye when we meet.

- Your opinions about the work we're doing matters, however, your repeated personal rants are borderline inappropriate.

- I don't appreciate that comment and I know others wouldn't either.

- Please refrain from sending me any more items not related to work.

- Remember, we work in a harassment-free place.

- Please don't use that language in the future.

- Obviously, inappropriate responses can occur, so be prepared. When someone curses at you, don't curse back. Respond in a calm and even-toned manner. If someone calls you a name, don't call them a name in response. When it comes to responding to inappropriate behavior, fighting fire with fire only serves to heighten the flames.

Managing awkward and uncomfortable conversations is not rocket-science, but it does require forethought. The suggested responses have worked for me however they may not work for everyone. Each situation is unique so feel free to adapt the suggested responses to language that feels appropriate for you and your situation. You must find what works for you. Every situation is different and the emotional beings behind the inappropriate behavior are different too. That's why I suggest practicing these statements out loud. Believing you can quickly and confidently respond to an uncomfortable situation in the moment is one thing. Actually responding is another. Practice will help you respond quickly and naturally to nip inappropriateness in the bud.

The very thing that will not work is embarrassment of any kind. Nothing shuts a person down or inflames them faster than embarrassment. Fighting fire with fire hurts an aggressor's pride and disturbs the balance of power, embarrassing them. They may throw it back at you ten times worse. Then you will truly have a target on your back.

THINK ABOUT IT

- Words can sting without leaving a physical mark. If they did not hurt, you'd be a cold-hearted robot. Then you'd have bigger things to worry about.

- Don't let the hurt sting for too long. Acknowledge your pain as legitimate but don't dwell on it or you'll create unnecessary negativity and rumination. It diverts your time and energy from life-giving experiences.

- Give yourself grace. You are a human who is not perfect—like everyone else.

- Practice bystander intervention to diffuse an abusive situation and change an environment.

- Remember, the goal is never to embarrass a harasser but to initiate change.

PUT IT TO WORK: DWIGHT WANTS TO BE LEFT ALONE

Dwight has worked in the insurance industry a long time, bouncing between a few corporations in an effort to move up the corporate ladder and make a bit more money. Dwight is a good worker and loyal team member who always participates in after-work happy hours and celebratory holiday gatherings. Most of his coworkers bring spouses to these events, but not Dwight. He is gay and not yet ready to share that aspect of his life with others, not even his family. He is sensitive about the issue and afraid of rejection.

Deb works with Dwight and shares her unsolicited opinions with everyone in earshot of her desk. She frequently gives coworkers personal criticism at inopportune times, such as team meetings, in an effort to garner attention or detract focus from her work. Deb runs into Dwight as he exits a local gay bar holding hands with his boyfriend, Casey. While Deb and Dwight exchange pleasantries, Deb glances at Dwight and Casey's tightly clutched hands. Dwight's head spins. Deb clearly understands that Dwight is gay. What is she going to do with her discovery?

Work in Dwight's department takes a turn when a new position opens. Dwight and Deb both vie for the job. Deb begins taking her tactics of embarrassment to new extremes with Dwight. She starts a rumor that Dwight has HIV because he is gay. She leaves pornographic LGBTQ-themed photos on Dwight's desk. She openly mocks Dwight in meetings and laughs at gay stereotypes and makes suggestive, hip-thrusting gestures and negative comments to or at Dwight in both public and private settings.

Dwight begins lying to cover up his homosexuality. That leads to shame, guilt, and anxiety. Ultimately, Dwight spends more time doing damage control with Deb than he does doing his work.

When Deb's inappropriate behavior establishes a negative attitude toward Dwight throughout the department, he asks her why she is taking such measures to intimidate him and hurt his reputation. Deb deflects the question. She claims she doesn't know what Dwight is talking about; he's simply being too sensitive and needs to lighten up.

ASSESS THE SITUATION

- Why would Dwight feel so guilty about this situation?

- What approach is best for Dwight in handling Deb's inappropriate behavior? What approach is best for the company?

- What rights does Dwight have in his workplace?

- What recourse does Dwight have in his workplace?

CHAPTER 6

THE REALITIES
OF SPEAKING OUT

> While sexual harassment can be described and supported with some statistics, what you won't find anywhere are the unquantifiable effects of this pervasive problem—the very personal losses of sexual harassment.

WHAT REALLY HAPPENS when someone speaks out about workplace harassment? Those who are brave enough to come forward are often targeted and face increased abuse. They may be ostracized or retaliated against. Although these reactions are somewhat obvious, they oversimplify the broader consequences. The reality of speaking out is complex, messy, and often deeply disruptive on an emotional level. Unfortunately, there's a widespread lack of understanding about the nature and impact of sexual harassment.

A 2003 United States Equal Employment Opportunity Commission study found that 75 percent of people who spoke up about sexual harassment were retaliated against.[5] While the EEOC notes that reported cases increased in 2018, 90 percent of harassed employees admit to never reporting. Those statistics come as no surprise as I continue to see headlines shedding light on toxic workplaces and hear from targets who fear retribution and worse.

I want those numbers to change. I want to make the world a better, friendlier place where an employee's only concern at work is putting forth their best effort. To spread the message, I'll speak to anyone who will listen. I advocate for best practices, legislative changes, and better personal support systems for targets, and I encourage others to do the same. If you'd asked me five years ago to speak at length about this topic publicly, I would have laughed in your face. Over time, I gained the confidence to speak out, loud and proud, about the realities of workplace harassment. Not everyone is able or willing to advocate in this way, so I'm sharing my personal knowledge to provide an alternative, reality-based perspective in a sea of conflicting messages. Targets are told to keep their heads down, continue on, just grin and bear it, or don't rock the boat—anything instead of speaking up and reporting. But that has to change.

Changing hearts and minds is an uphill battle. Some people are simply jerks who will never change. That's reality of the world we live in. But humans are fundamentally good, well-intentioned, and loving beings. Sharing my message has drawn an outpouring of love, support, and acceptance from people of all walks of life, from men and women. As humans, we truly have more similarities than we do differences.

There is no single word to define sexual harassment. It's a game of power, an abusive set of circumstances that can affect the target both physically and mentally. It harms the spirit in ways unique to each individual. It occurs in a wide variety of situations and creates resentment, self-doubt, depression, anxiety, fear, anger, shame, embarrassment, and more. Its nebulous character creates frustration and confusion and a myriad of opinions.

The dictionary tells us that sexual harassment is, "Uninvited and unwelcome verbal or physical behavior of a sexual nature, especially by a person in authority toward a subordinate (such as an employee or student)." Court cases and preferred best practice procedures help interpret the meaning further. Consider these words from the US Equal Employment Opportunity Commission, the federal office that enforces anti-discriminatory laws:

> *It is unlawful to harass a person (an applicant or employee) because of that person's sex. Harassment can include "sexual harassment" or unwelcome sexual advances, requests for sexual favors, and other verbal or physical harassment of a sexual nature.*
>
> *Harassment does not have to be of a sexual nature, however, and can include offensive remarks about a person's sex. For example, it is illegal to harass a woman by making offensive comments about women in general.*
>
> *Both victim and the harasser can be either a woman or a man, and the victim and harasser can be the same sex.*
>
> *Although the law doesn't prohibit simple teasing, offhand comments, or isolated incidents that are not very serious, harassment is illegal when it is so frequent or severe that it creates a hostile or offensive work environment or when it results in an adverse employment decision (such as the victim being fired or demoted).*
>
> *The harasser can be the victim's supervisor, a supervisor in another area, a coworker, or someone who is not an employee of the employer, such as a client or customer.*[6]

UNQUANTIFIABLE EFFECTS

While sexual harassment can be described and supported with some statistics, what you won't find anywhere are the unquantifiable effects of this pervasive problem—the very personal losses of sexual harassment. These are consequences that scientists cannot study, measure, or even accurately identify, let alone understand, due to the devastating emotional and psychological toll it takes:

1. **Self-perception and self-worth.** At one point I thought so poorly of myself that I struggled to function from day to day. I dreamed for years about unrealistic, unhealthy scenarios related to being the office hero who was praised endlessly for my "amazing" work. That unrealistic view of myself and my workplace damaged my well-being.

2. **Darkness or depression.** The severe hatred boiling in my heart manifested physically with headaches and lack of energy and appetite. I cried gallons of tears, sometimes daily and most often privately. I devoted too much time and mental space to revenge. Old scenarios played over and over again in my head, and I obsessed over how I could and should have handled them differently. I was clinically depressed. It was hard to do or accomplish anything. My mental state turned me into a critical, snarky, person my husband did not like to spend time with. I didn't want to spend time with myself, because I'd start cycling through negative self-talk and anger-focused narratives about feeling trapped.

3. **Job prospects.** My deplorable, demeaning work situation had me struggling career-wise. Throughout the entire five-year period of my employment at the Iowa Legislature, I applied for other jobs hoping for an exit. I looked for work that would provide an advancement in status and title, jobs that would help me keep my career on trajectory. I went on many unsuccessful interviews. I'm not surprised I didn't get those jobs. I no doubt radiated an air of desperation and negativity because I was no longer confident about myself or my ability to do good and impactful work.

4. **Lost sense of empowerment.** Before working at the Iowa Legislature, I took pride in my ability to provide effective and efficient communications that impacted others, but that was not the case after

years of sexual harassment and bullying. After being told repeatedly that I was not good enough, not trusted; and should only do, say, and wear what certain people thought I should; I was a shell of who I used to be. I hated myself for it.

Many other possible losses occur as a result of speaking out, including productivity; trust; a sense of stability, identity, and belonging; career trajectory; social circles; relationships of all kinds; and enjoyment of life.

Often, targets cut their losses and move on just to escape, even if it means taking a lateral position, a pay cut or loss of salary if another position cannot be secured immediately. Unfortunately, an interrupted or stagnated career takes years to rebuild, and it's more likely to happen to women than men.

DEBUNKING MISGUIDED NOTIONS

How often do we make judgement calls over situations we know nothing about?

All the time!

"Just tell the abuser to knock it off," is one of those judgmental phrases that people have no business stating to anyone. Why? Because it's never that simple. I hear the, "Knock it off," statement from people who don't know much about workplace harassment, people who have never experienced or witnessed it. They certainly have not experienced the confrontation and messiness that results. "Just tell them to knock it off," might only make the situation worse.

Let me help you to peel back the layers on this onion of a topic by debunking some commonly held, misguided notions that range from mildly annoying to wildly inaccurate. Too often, they're used as an easy way out, even though they're not aligned with the reality of modern-day workplaces.

1. **Telling the abuser to "knock it off" is never enough to solve the problem.** First, confrontation is hard. Unless you are prepared to face your harasser and follow through with bravery and accountability, this action is difficult to execute. What does a person do after telling an abuser to knock it off, to stop, that enough is enough? It's a slippery slope leading to despair and frustration because telling someone to stop only goads them on.

   In my experience, abuse worsens because "Knock it off" leaves the behavior unchecked. Standing up to my bully only fueled his fire to find something cruder and more embarrassing to say that would make me and my coworkers squirm. It took a lawsuit and several years after I was fired for my harasser to be shown the door. Harassers don't want to be embarrassed in front of others. They want to be seen as funny and engaging, the life of the party, the center of attention—especially in a workplace setting. They want to exhibit their power and control over others, reinforcing the idea they can do whatever they want, free from consequences.

   Rarely do we hear of an abuser who is required to make a remorseful apology and then proceeded to alter their behavior in a positive way. This speaks to the idiom, "Jerks will always be jerks." I still have hope that some jerks out there realize the error of their ways and feel badly about making others uncomfortable. Those instances are few and far between. Let's face it, people don't really want to change who they are, let alone their habits and tendencies. The reality is that they don't believe they did anything wrong.

2. **Human resource departments aren't just out to protect the company, the CEO, and their reputations**. I'm here to defend HR professionals. I know of and have worked with many of them. Human resource pros have a tough a job dealing with all things people-related. That's a broad mandate. It can mean anything from handling salary reviews and increases to being the fashion police enforcing a dress code.

Human resources often mean different things within different organizations too. When I worked in the Iowa Legislature, there wasn't an HR person on staff. Instead, a payroll person was tasked to complete a few HR items like ensuring employees received information about their benefits. My immediate bosses were responsible for updating staff about health benefit changes and pay scale information, among other things.

Commonly, small organizations don't have a dedicated person for HR-related tasks. The overhead and salary for an HR position can be more than many small and growing businesses can afford. Human resource services generally fall to a designated employee, someone who often has no background in the field.

Dealing with people can be difficult, so HR is arguably one of the toughest jobs in any workplace. Implementing hiring practices is hard. Keeping up with pay scales is hard. Ensuring raises, promotions, and benefits are effectively managed is hard. Ensuring company culture, policies and procedures are continually updated is hard.

Have there been many documented instances where HR professionals worked to push out or eliminate employees who have been harassed, bullied or worse at work? Yes. Many times, HR workers need to keep their jobs just as much as the employees who have been abused. Is it a terrible disservice to those who lose jobs after coming forward for legitimate reasons? Yes. Is it fair? No. Politics and power imbalances still run rampant in our society and culture. These disparities sometimes pressure seemingly good HR pros into siding with abusive CEOs and high performers. It's not a widespread conspiracy. It's simply what our culture has perpetuated as a practice. If we want to break the cycle, we must collectively continue the conversation. We need to encourage workplaces to implement best practices and eliminate the harasser for workplace welfare.

3. **Targets can't solve the problem by simply leaving their situations and finding another job.** An endless number of factors drive employees' decisions to stay in an abusive or terrible situation. The biggest factor is employment. If a person doesn't have another job to jump into, they cannot earn money. If there are few jobs in their community or surrounding area, leaving a bad situation is even trickier. If a person's background prohibits them from finding new employment, the situation grows even more complex. Finally, community plays a large role. Whether big or small, industry-related or peer-driven, communities impact decisions. Rumors and gossip within those communities are damaging to a person's reputation and can contribute to a new employer's decision to hire or not.

   In addition to the security of an existing job, targets are often reluctant to leave the job-related benefits they receive. There is a reason companies spend lots of money on retaining employees with wellness programs, food and drink provisions at work, and ancillary benefits your grandparents would never have conceived as part of the workplace. It's always more cost-effective for the organization to keep their employees in place. According to a University of California at Berkeley study, on average, it costs $4,000 above salary and wages to hire a new employee. That figure rises to $7,000 for replacing management-level employees and professionals. A 2017 Training Industry report showed that it costs small companies, on average, $1,886 to train new employees. These are simply a few examples of cost-driven decision-making.[7]

4. **Women are NOT out to get men!** Unfortunately, the idea that all men should be frightened about accusations of bad behavior is running rampant. It's so extreme that, in response to the #MeToo movement, some men are refusing to mentor women.

   To think women are out to get men is a dangerous, destructive idea that should be put to rest. Only 2 percent of accusations of sexual harassment are proven to be false.[8] It's still okay for men to mentor women. Women want to be treated equally, which includes fair pay so they can provide for their families and be respected. It's not a tough concept to grasp. This lame excuse to avoid mentoring women arises frequently these days. I call *bull* each time. There are equal numbers of men and women in the workplace, but there are more men in positions of power. There are very few female C-Suite executives. The numbers are growing but it will take time.

If men are good, fair, and respectful toward others, they have nothing to worry about. If you are a man who is worried about this, take an honest, humbling look at how you have interacted with co-workers in the past. Think about those interactions and ask yourself if someone has cause to accuse you of something. What are you afraid of?

We must have men in on this conversation. We must have men who are willing to mentor women, to be advocates and allies for us until we level the playing field. Allowing men to retreat from these responsibilities is a setback we should continue to address in an open and honest way.

5. **Top performers who abuse other staff are (generally) protected by their employers.** Although this is not universal, it largely remains true. Their productivity, high sales performance, or a personal relationship with a board member or business owner gives them the leverage they need to keep their positions. As power imbalances are exposed in various organizations at multiple levels, we see a historical trend to show the harassed employees the door rather than remove that noxious CEO or salesman-of-the-year. There is a legitimate fear among targets that their employers will not believe their accounts.

Not ridding an organization of a toxic employee is wrong from moral and financial perspectives Let's do a cost-benefit analysis:

- Cost in annual lost productivity wages (per employee) with continued harassment: $8,800[9]

- Average salary of a sales executive: $254,000[10] versus the average salary of an entry level position with college degree: $51,000[11]

- Average lawyer fees to litigate a sexual harassment trial: $200 per hour,[12] potentially costing millions

- Average sexual harassment settlement: $54,651[13]

- Cost in damaged company reputation: priceless

Eliminating an employee who wreaks havoc on the workforce with unacceptable behavior is always a more cost-effective route than keeping a toxic top-performer on staff.

People who come forward and speak their truth about sexual harassment often have nothing left to lose. The hard realities of speaking out are sometimes outweighed by a target's desire to simply get their life back. That's exactly what I wanted after I was fired. I wanted to go to work and just do work. I wanted a sense of comfort and confidence. Of mental well-being and normalcy.

As bystanders we must do a better job of helping others create normalcy. Standing up against inappropriate behavior is a good starting point. Resist the urge to look the other way because you feel embarrassed or awkward, and certainly avoid judging anyone at any time. As the saying goes, everyone you meet is fighting a battle you know nothing about.[14] When people offer grace, understanding, and respect to another, the world becomes a better place. Workplaces are better, and people are better. The harsh realities of speaking out are scary. When we can show a bit more decency toward one another, everyone benefits.

THINK ABOUT IT

- What has been lost can be found again. Talking about unquantifiable losses normalizes such conversations. It's meaningful and helpful to recovery.

- Don't think of losses as barriers, but rather doors that have momentarily closed. They can be opened again.

- Hard work matters; being respected matters. If you don't receive respect in your workplace, you should work elsewhere.

- Misconceptions are everywhere and there is never one easy answer. Know that circumstances are more complicated than that.

PUT IT TO WORK:
PENNY'S REALITY

Dan is the company's top performer and a well-connected guy who is out and about in the community frequently. Not only is Dan the top performer and a friend of the CEO, he was recently named Employee of the Year. Despite that honor, he continually disrespects others in the office.

Penny has been Dan's administrative assistant for ten years. She usually bears the brunt of his aggression. When Dan doesn't make a sale, he typically blames Penny. He calls her names and asks personal questions about her relationship with her partner, who just happens to be of the same sex. Sometimes Dan will draw pictures or show Penny photographs of sex acts to see her reaction. Other times Dan tells her various dirty jokes and asks her to choose which one would be the most appropriate to share with the company's Board of Directors.

Penny does not have a college education. She and her partner have three children, and her partner is a contract social worker who also works part-time at the local bookstore to make some extra money. Thanks to Penny's job, the family has a good benefits package which includes health care coverage and a 401(k). In their town, there are few office jobs available with benefits.

Penny does not like her job, but she puts up with Dan's psychological abuse because it pays well and provides health benefits. If she stands up to Dan or reports his behavior to the HR department, she is afraid she will lose her position, status, and title. Year after year, Penny has let it go.

ASSESS THE SITUATION

- How is this job affecting Penny's mental and physical health?

- Do you think Penny's experience at work affects her roles as a mother, spouse, and worker?

- Do you think Dan realizes he is disrespecting Penny?

- Should Penny speak to Dan about his behavior?

- After ten years, do you think others in this workplace know what Penny is experiencing?

- What should the coworkers in this workplace do or say to Dan about his treatment of Penny?

- Should the Board of Directors know about Dan's bad behavior?

- How would the company be affected if Dan left?

- Who would be more affected by work disruption or rumors in their small town: Dan or Penny?

CHAPTER 7

TRAVERSING THE EMOTIONAL MOUNTAIN

> The messy emotional weight strapped to my back continued to pull me down after each steep step I took up that mountain until I finally realized I needed a hiking pole to steady myself.

FEAR, SHAME, AND guilt are complex and confusing emotions that play a prominent role in the lives of targets. They place a mountain of emotional obstacles between us and forward movement. Fear of losing a job. Fear of being publicly mocked or degraded. Shame over being a punching bag for others. Shame for not having the courage to speak out about it. And guilt over the burden of being a target and not wanting to saddle others with their problems, thinking they can do nothing about it.

Living under a mountain of fear, shame, and guilt is all-consuming. I made every effort to project an image of professionalism and strength, pretending that I could handle any situation that came my way. I felt strongly that no one needed to know my business, including the fact that I was being sexually harassed and bullied daily. Fear and shame over the abuse made me feel disingenuous; I wasn't living the way I projected myself to be. I felt guilty about holding onto a secret I didn't want my family to know. I was struggling, yet I didn't want to burden anyone else with my problems. Everyone has enough problems of their own, I reasoned.

The messy emotional weight strapped to my back continued to pull me down after each steep step I took up that mountain until I finally realized I needed a hiking pole to steady myself. Only then, only when I invited the support I needed, did I relinquish the secrecy. Telling my family about what was going on was liberating. So was their acknowledgement that I had been unfairly pushed into a terrible position by an abuser. Those realizations helped me trek out from under the emotional burden and over the mountain it created.

I hope reading about my experience helps you see the ridiculousness of silence, of withholding your truth. A fresh perspective, time, and speaking openly can provide immense healing for you, just as it did for me.

Being self-aware—paying attention to our emotions and what they are trying to tell us—helps us to move toward healing. The whole spectrum of emotions are part of everyday life. They can't be avoided. It's up to us to figure out how to navigate the obstacles placed in our way, and we don't have to do it alone.

FEAR OF SPEAKING UP

Let's face it: most people don't want to speak up because they fear negative consequences, from being judged unfairly by others to being fired. A short five years ago, speaking to the public with truth and honesty about sexual harassment was considered taboo. It's no wonder the US Equal Employment Opportunity Commission states that 90 percent of sexual harassment incidences are not reported.[15] That's telling. Thankfully, the tide is turning.

When I made the decision to speak out, I was afraid of judgement, however, the desire to free myself from continual fear, shame, and guilt propelled me forward. Later, when my situation came to light, I let my extended family know what was going on. One fairly close relative did not respond. I did not hear a peep from them. No words of reassurance, not a phone call, not even a brief email letting me know they were thinking of me in a tough time.

Fast forward a few years. Right after my case was settled, I went to dinner with this relative. They asked point blank, "Well, was it all worth it? For the money you got?"

Something in their tone implied my singular motivation was money. I angrily replied, "It was never about the money. Never."

And the reply I got was, "Well, you never would've survived the '80s." With those words, they proceeded to pass judgement on me, insinuating I wasn't tough enough and that they had suffered far worse in 1980s corporate America.

You can imagine how this angered and disappointed me. There is no competition for who has been harassed the most in life. I don't want to out-shame anyone with stories of the lewd and disgusting behavior I endured. No one wins a prize for the most egregious thing that ever happened to them. I don't share my story to evoke pity. I share it so others can learn from it.

I later found out my relative didn't realize their comment had been hurtful and unsupportive. They had distanced themselves from me because my situation triggered fear, shame, and guilt in their own life over experiences they weren't yet ready to deal with. They never moved past the fear of speaking up. That left them ill-equipped to provide the support I wanted and needed, so they backed away and inadvertently lashed out while also passing judgement.

Judgement is just one more punch to the downtrodden. If your thoughts are needed, you'll be asked for them, and remember, you can't know the inner battle preventing someone else from making healthy choices. Those who are ill-equipped to respond in a helpful, supportive way are often dealing with their own emotional mountain climb. It's easier to offer judgement instead and brush trauma aside.

In all fairness, I never voiced the support I wanted and needed from my family because I didn't know how to ask for it, just as my relative didn't know how to talk about their own triggering situation. Personally, I didn't know *what* to ask for, partly because I didn't know what lay ahead in my legal battle. I only asked friends for prayer right before the trial started—a bit late in the game, but by that point, I had a better understanding of what I needed in the moment.

Speaking up is no longer awkward for me I know when and how to ask for support and what to ask for. I've discussed my own emotional mess so often that I no longer feel ashamed or guilty about what happened to me. I'm no longer embarrassed to call attention to myself, hold others accountable, and call out bad behavior.

NURTURING EMPATHY

We spend years educating ourselves about practical things like mathematics, history, civics, health, and biology. We spend no time teaching people how to have tough conversations, how to share feelings appropriately, how to ask for help, how to truly listen to others, how to share wants and needs, and how to appropriately govern workplace interactions. These soft skills are fundamental to getting ahead in life!

I was brought up with the attitude, "If you have nothing nice to say, say nothing at all." That was my lesson. I went into the workplace after college as a shy and wide-eyed thing, ready to work hard no matter what, and ready to keep anything that wasn't nice to myself.

Working hard is good, but it isn't enough. We need to learn how to be empathetic to one another and nurture it in our relationships. One way to do that is to revive the art of civil conversation and incorporate it into our lives. That includes listening as well as speaking out about what's right. Speaking out is particularly difficult for women, who are automatically labeled as shrill, annoying, or bitchy when we speak up and try to share our emotions—even when we use a respectful tone of voice.

We have to kick those labels to the curb. Too often, it's easier to avoid talking about circumstances than to deal with the fallout. We have to change the collective mindset about discussing tough and important topics because it matters. People who've experienced harassment deserve dialogue. When you stand up with or for someone else or yourself, it makes a difference. It leads to change.

That does not mean it's easy. The #MeToo movement, originating in 2006 and revived in 2017,[16] has done wonders for targets by creating a sense of shared experiences. More people have felt comfortable coming forward. In 2019, the U.S. Equal Employment Opportunity Commission reported that sexual harassment civil trials and settlements had increased roughly 60 percent from the previous year.[17] There are still real, tangible consequences in speaking out. They send fear into the heart of targets, but make no mistake, there is freedom in speaking up. Speaking up can take you to the top of that mountain of fear, shame, and guilt.

Once the crest of the mountain is traversed, you'll encounter a breathtaking moment. It's the split second after your truths tumble out of your mouth, that instant before the person you're speaking with responds. It's a *what now* pause, the moment of change. What comes next can push you over the edge or send you safely and slowly hiking down the other side. It all depends upon how the party you're speaking to responds to your truth.

Sometimes that moment of change is lost on the receiving party. Sometimes the pause hits them squarely in the face, imposing a burden they must respond to. Typically, they're taken off guard. In any case, they probably aren't equipped to handle what they're hearing. They may respond poorly to the detriment of the individual sharing emotionally sensitive information, and to the business involved. It's a misstep that is far harder to rectify after the fact. It's vitally important to get that moment of change right for more than just the targets.

My moment of change happened when I was fired with no explanation or warning. The shock left me numb and wondering, *what now?* Even though my lawyer had explained beforehand what might result from submitting my memo of complaint, I had clung to hope. I was convinced my employer would want to work with me to change the office environment. But they didn't, and that changed everything.

Climbing the inevitable mountain of emotions that result from a *what now* moment is doable. I did it, and I survived to come down the other side. I'm here to tell you that regardless of what happens afterward, climbing up and over that mountain is an admirable thing. If and when someone confronts their fear, speaks up, and encounters that *what now* pause it is not a failure. It's a step forward, and that's a huge accomplishment. The workplace may not change as a result, but the person who speaks out is stronger and forever changed.

The world would be a different and better place if all humans were more empathetic. If they were, it would be easier to feel remorseful for wrongdoing and take responsibility for those wrongs. Remorse is a feeling anyone can bounce back from if it isn't construed as shame. Targets yearn for their abusers' remorse.

IMPORTANCE OF REMORSE

Remorse occurs when an aggressor recognizes the wrong they committed and the hurt they caused. Remorse means feeling actual guilt and regret over a situation. Unfortunately, remorse isn't common, often because there isn't enough empathy going around to trigger it.

On a sunny spring afternoon when I still worked at the Iowa legislature, a freshman senator sauntered up to me and two of my male co-workers, one of whom was my boss.

"Hey, I'm back from lunch and ready to debate. Who should I call on to ask my questions on this bill?" He looked directly at me, slurring his questions, wreaking of booze.

"We're recessed right now," I said, "We'll gavel back in soon and debate those bills from the morning."

He suddenly became agitated, as if a switch had been flipped. His face contorted in anger. "Who are you to tell me what to do? Who do you think you are?" he declared.

"I don't understand. I'm not sure I know what you're talking about," I said, shocked at his aggression.

"What? You think you're better than me, don't you?" His body tensed and he stepped toward me as if ready for a fight.

"What? I don't get it." I stepped back.

"You think you're Queen Latifah! You're SO high and mighty! So much better than anyone! You're being ridiculous," He rambled on, waving his arms and swaying.

I was not the lone witness of his aggression. Two other people stood with me. Many bystanders occupied the chamber as well. Yet no one told this man to stop shouting at me or attempted to divert his attention. No one pulled him aside to the men's room, a mere twenty-five feet away. No one intervened. In that moment of utter loneliness, I longed for someone to acknowledge what had just transpired, to ask if I was okay. The incident was never referred to, at least not with me, and to my knowledge, no one said anything to the disrespectful senator. If such matters are kept silent, bad behavior is condoned. How can a person be remorseful if they don't believe their behavior is wrong? The conversation never begins. We have to become comfortable saying something, anything, to stand up for ourselves and for one another.

On Thursday, October 4, 2018, the Governor of Iowa stated publicly that workplace harassment is a bad thing and issued a proclamation declaring October to be Change the Culture Month. The governor said, "Throughout history, sexual harassment has been a stain on our culture. It is a destructive force in the workplace and in all facets of life."

I could not agree more. The full proclamation can be found on the State of Iowa website.[18]

Proclamations are good for drawing attention to or away from something and not much more. While a proclamation may lean toward empathy, without legislation and consequences to back it up, it shows no remorse, rendering it ineffective.

This proclamation was akin to telling an aggressor *we want you to know that we don't like what you're doing* but we're throwing our hands in the air and looking the other way when something bad happens. To say leaders who don't back up what they say with accountability are a disappointment is an understatement.

ESTABLISHING ACCOUNTABILITY

Workplace systems and procedures accommodate and protect the harasser. Unfortunately, the system is based upon the common misconception that the target is the one creating unnecessary drama and making inconvenient demands. As a result, when sexual harassment occurs, the target is pushed aside or even discounted. They are moved to another department or fired. When and if settlements or judgements are granted, they usually arrive in the form of money, which does not fix the problem. The abuser can move somewhere else, potentially harming others and damaging another workplace.

Why do we let this never-ending cycle of power and control for the abuser continue? We need to take a more empathic view of these situations.

Let's shift our collective mindset and view harassers as the perpetrators of workplace drama. Let's hold them accountable. They are the ones creating any inconvenience. They throw disrespect around freely and care little about how others feel. They perceive they wield all the workplace power, that they are untouchable. But that couldn't be further from the truth. If we view workplace harassment from an empathetic perspective, the entire conversation shifts.

Along with a conversational shift must come stiffer consequences for abusers. Consequences are necessary to hold them accountable, and accountability must be present at all times for understanding and change to occur. That will result in a reduction of lawsuits and settlements as well as overall incidences of inappropriateness. This also means accountability measures must be clearly stated up front in every workplace, frequently discussed, and understood by all.

As each person and situation varies, so should consequences and accountability. Finding what works will take something akin to negotiation. Wage garnishment, mandatory counseling and training, community service—whatever it might take to get an abuser to see they have a problem and that they hurt others. We can no longer shy away from this. Real and tangible consequences enforce change.

We need accountability in the halls where our laws are made. That means leaders must step up to discuss, promote and pass legislation that works for and protects employees, providing more guidance and support. We need leaders at every level to take the issue seriously. They must take steps to eradicate inappropriate behavior on the spot and reinforce consequences through accountability. We need change in board rooms, break rooms, and back rooms through leadership, support, and action.

While I completely agree with the statement the governor issued on that day in October, I had hoped she would at least mention actionable items, accountability, and consequences. She did not. Even though my case was highly publicized and likely at least partly responsible for the proclamation, I was not consulted or invited to the proclamation ceremony. No follow-up has resulted from the proclamation—no committees established, annual reviews or audits enacted, and no additional discussions heard from leaders in power.

Over the last few years, I've worked with lawmakers on substantive legislation only to see it die in subcommittee. It doesn't discourage me, however, and I will continue to work with state legislators who are willing to enact change. Only time will tell if governments back up their rhetoric with action.

As I work to enact concrete change, I still hear little about remorse, which says a lot about how much and how often we empathize. Remorse and empathy are closely aligned. Harassment and bullying are forms of abuse and those who abuse others rarely admit fault. They tend to dig into denial and turn every situation into a "he said, she said" dilemma. Those are the worst types of situations. They are always emotionally charged and generally have little supporting documentation or evidence. Civility and decorum often unravel quickly. It's absolutely heartbreaking to hear and hard to watch play out.

The September 2018 US Senate Judiciary Committee hearing into accusations of assault against vetted Supreme Court nominee Brett Kavanaugh was proof of that. By all accounts, the majority of Americans were riveted to Dr. Christine Blasey-Ford's testimony against Kavanaugh. He had been accused with a serious allegation of assault and a violation of bodily autonomy. The hearing turned into a classic case of "he said, she said," where empathy was definitely not in play. Both Ford and Kavanaugh were 100 percent certain in their accounts: she said it happened, he said it didn't. Ford gave tempered and well-measured accounts of the assault. Kavanaugh took a dramatic, tearful, and partisan approach to his testimony. Their accounts and how they were delivered will be scrutinized and studied for years to come.

Despite the deadlocked proceedings, Dr. Ford's testimony was empowering for hundreds of thousands of women throughout the country.

It shed light on the impact of suppressed trauma memory and the bravery associated with coming forward.

During Dr. Ford's testimony, the National Sexual Assault Hotline experienced a 201% increase in calls in one day and a 338% increase during a four-day period.[19] Thousands of women stood up and spoke out about their assaults and why they chose to stay silent, prompting the hashtag, #WhyIDidntReport. It sparked a national debate about victim believability and the current high cost of coming forward with accusations against men. We can bring that cost down by continuing these discussions in order to normalize the conversation, making everyone more comfortable with the topic.

This national debate also sheds light on why so many women carry the shame and guilt associated with traumatic experiences. There are too many lingering misconceptions associated with inappropriate behavior and how we process what we hear from the abused and abuser. Some women still feel they should have prevented the abuse in some way. Maybe if they had not been drinking. Maybe if they had been nicer to the perpetrator. Maybe if they had worn less revealing clothing. Targets linger in the what if's and live with the guilt and shame of situations that aggressive, power-hungry brutes thrust upon them.

After the verdict for my harassment suit was announced, arrangements for the settlement were made by a former Iowa senator—a woman I had once worked for who eventually left the Iowa Senate to serve as the Lieutenant Governor. Later, she became the governor who issued the Change the Culture proclamation. At no time did she offer any personal show of support or remorse for what she witnessed me go through. This woman knew me. We had worked together. Here was a woman in a position of power with a remarkable opportunity to stand up for all women in the state, to show that human decency, care, and support were alive and well. Instead, she chose silence.

Getting abusers to apologize or take any accountability for their actions is rare. That leaves most targets in a vengeful state and makes it difficult to climb out from under fear, shame, and guilt. In my situation, men and women in positions of political power—people I worked closely with, whose families I knew—had the opportunity to at least denounce inappropriate behavior. They did not. I cannot emphasize enough how hurtful that was. It drove me to dig in, fight harder, and eventually share my lessons learned in these pages.

THINK ABOUT IT

- The release of fear, shame and guilt is an important step in a healing journey.

- Nurturing empathy creates a capacity for remorse and greater potential for holding people accountable for their actions. It's worth the effort.

- What kinds of consequences for bad behavior might demonstrate accountability in your workplace?

- How can you reinforce consequences in your environment?

PUT IT TO WORK:
DEVIN IS THE CENTER OF ATTENTION

Devin strives to be the center of attention, a prankster who never takes himself or anyone else too seriously. He always tells jokes, no matter the situation. Devin feeds off the energy in the office, so he enjoys telling stories and tall tales to get reactions. He has worked at the office long enough to know what his co-workers find funny and what they find offensive, but he seems to enjoy pushing boundaries and telling embarrassing stories.

Devin's colleagues know his behavior borders on harassment, but he has always been careful about what he says in front of his bosses. They have never reprimanded him.

Most often, Devin's jokes are directed at the newest member of the team, someone with little ability to impose consequences or demand accountability. Newer employees don't know how to respond to Devin's behavior, so they try to ignore him and stay out of his way.

Bobby recently joined the staff and sits at the desk next to Devin's. True to form, Devin switched his attention from the last newcomer to Bobby. He took special pleasure in cracking jokes about Bobby's wheelchair or asking personal, insensitive questions about his disability. Being the new person, Bobby allowed Devin's behavior to slide for a short time—until it impeded his work. The jokes were so bothersome and insensitive that Bobby can't concentrate to complete his tasks. He can't stop Devin from talking, and he can't stay silent any longer.

ASSESS THE SITUATION

- How do you think Bobby should handle Devin?

- What are some positive and reinforcing words Bobby could use in a crucial conversation with Devin?

- How can Bobby hold Devin accountable for stopping the negative talk?

- How can Devin be a positive force in his organization?

- Is there a way Bobby can help others in the office let go of negativity and build trust?

- How can tangible consequences play a role in this scenario?

CHAPTER 8

THE RESPECT FACTOR

> Respect has less value than it once did. It takes too much time to earn respect or dole it out in a world that has come to value instant gratification and social media one-upmanship.

THERE SEEMS TO be a nationwide shortage of respect and a propensity to lay blame anywhere but on oneself. It's easier to place blame than to own something. This realization may be slightly jaded, but it's shaped by my own experience and by that of those who reach out for my advice or coaching on how to handle difficult situations. I spend a great deal of time talking to targets who have experienced situations similar to mine. They struggle to keep their heads above water. They fall into various stages of the harassment spectrum with experiences that range from being the subject of lewd and annoying jokes to being hit on repeatedly by an untouchable top performer. After rebuffing disrespectful talk or advances, they were fired. Even worse, some were physically assaulted at their place of employment. When they spoke up, they were fired.

Each situation reflects a striking breakdown in the currency of respect and the way people treat one another. Respect has less value than it once did. It takes too much time to earn respect or dole it out in a world that has come to value instant gratification and social media one-up-manship. The practice of flinging barbs has bled into life off-screen too, leaving many young adults reporting increased feelings of isolation in a world of social media connectedness.

How do we make better connections to maintain a sense of safety and engagement at work and in the world when people's attitudes toward respect are declining? I don't have an answer for this, but we have to do better and keep trying.

THE DAMAGE OF DISRESPECT

I learned the importance of respect at a young age. My mother lovingly jokes that I was born talking. I have always been a communicator with the gift of gab, and it drives my family crazy from time to time. In fifth grade, my American History Class studied a unit combining a mock trial with a historical reenactment. Everyone was assigned the role of a historical figure and given a script to portray that figure answering some of history's greatest questions. After much rehearsal, we completed the assignment by showcasing the reenactment for parents at the Middle School Spring Open House.

I was assigned the part of a lawyer questioning Abraham Lincoln about his decisions regarding slavery and the Civil War. The class developed the questions together to help create an overarching historical narrative. I knew what the questions were, and I knew what the answers of my classmate, Abraham Lincoln, would be because we practiced in class. There weren't supposed to be any surprises.

The night of the Spring Open House came, and our class proceeded to act out various historical scenarios. Everything went well for me and Honest Abe until I made an impulsive decision to go off-script and asked a random question of Mr. Lincoln. I have no recollection of the question but do remember the instant I made the decision to improvise, and I recall with vivid clarity what happened after. My classmate's eyes widened into a look of horror and her mouth fell open. I had caught her totally off guard. To her credit, she remained in character and did the best she could to respond by mumbling a quiet, almost indecipherable response, ending the scene.

The audience reacted exactly how I hoped they would: with astonishment, laughter, and undivided attention. My surprise question flipped the script, and I made sure to ask it with appropriate dramatic flair. Unfortunately, my teacher and classmate didn't share the audience's appreciation. I had disrespected them both by forcing them to improvise. I apologized to my teacher and classmate afterward and, thankfully, we all moved on.

Like plenty of other people, I was taught that going off-script in life is bad. It certainly was bad in my antics with the Lincoln skit! Typically, staying on-script for life means getting an education or learning a skill and then using that education or skill. When an unexpected event happens or circumstances accidently veer off-script, chaos ensues. We don't know how to react. The uncertainty of these off-script situations, however, is what makes or breaks us. Our reactions define us, and help makes us stronger, better, and more adaptable.

Being disrespected at work threw me off my script. It was especially hurtful because I identified as a career woman on track for advancement and leadership positions. I worked hard and had high hopes. My career was a part of my identity. I chose to complete college and graduate one semester early to get a jump on the crowded job market. While in high school, I took college courses to ensure an early college graduation. This was the type of dedication I resigned myself to as a working woman. I wanted into the career club and all the respect that came with it for my efforts. That was my script.

Disrespect and sexual harassment were hard for me to grasp. It threw me off-script in a big way. It chipped away at my psyche. It unfolded so gradually that I didn't understand what was happening for a long time. Only after I was fired did I realize how much my script mattered to me and how damaging disrespect could be. I had worked hard to build up my reputation as someone who did good and reputable work. To me, good work was equivalent to automatic respect.

RESPECT SHOULD MATTER TO EVERYONE

While we should freely extend respect to others as a general expression of human relationship, professional respect is earned. I have always believed that hard work will win the day and good work will shine through mediocrity. Put time and effort into tasks—big, small, and in-between. No job is too big or small for anyone who is willing to learn.

Although I still believe the equilibrium of that statement, the current political tenor of the US has deteriorated dramatically and contributed to a growing worldwide disregard for respect. Those in elected office feel free to bully and ridicule others publicly with no regard for truth or consequences, giving civilians license to do the same. National politics used to employ passive aggressiveness and veiled threats. The behavior, comments, and opinions were less personal and more pragmatic. Nowadays, personal attacks are the common currency. The louder and meaner the discourse, the seemingly more effective.

A 2019 USA Today study showed that President Donald J. Trump increased the use of negative words in his tweets as well as words with angry connotations.[20] Much of this could be attributed to current events and increased public scrutiny, but it does not excuse the behavior in any way. When a president goes off script and is continuously disrespectful, any sense of ethical leadership dissolves, and you know you're in trouble. The same study found a decrease in President Trump's tweets conveying trust and joy. At a time when we need to choose our words carefully in an effort to build trust and spread joy, the most powerful commander in the world was sowing seeds of negativity and distrust.

We have to do better. We have to cultivate more respect and encourage others to do the same. We have to teach our children they can and should rise above negativity and distrust to be more respectful to everyone, regardless of who they are or what positions they hold.

My brother is a chef at a grocery store. He interacts with many customers daily and plans workshops to help them make their own meals. Sadly, he ends up being a punching bag for those who are frustrated with the store, the food, or whatever is bothering them that day. I was surprised to hear that he encountered so much negativity. He said, "You'd be surprised what happens when the customer is always right."

Those who work in the service industry are most easily abused because they are in front of people constantly. They often depend on tips to make a living because they earn very little in hourly pay. They face a tremendous amount of disrespect. The phrase, "The customer is always right," is a damaging lie. The customer can be a hurtful enemy of the barista, bartender, or server who simply wants to provide service. Do accidents happen? Can service workers have bad or "off" days? Absolutely, but that is no excuse to take rage or anger out on another person. No one deserves to be a punching bag, to put up with inappropriate, lewd, suggestive, or disgusting talk and behavior. Verbal abuse has no place in our society. It's the ultimate expression of disrespect.

I spend time traveling and attending conferences attended by other professionals. I speak at these conferences and educate attendees about the complexities of workplace harassment and the far-reaching damage that occurs when organizations choose a reactive versus proactive approach. Respect always comes into play. Inevitably, I end up chatting about it at length with conference-goers. I often get questions about how to educate our kids on the subject. For many, teaching an older, disrespectful coworker a new way of working seems more than tough and not worth the time. (By the way, teaching "old dogs" new tricks is doable—and worth it.)

So why not start off with the younger crowd? I've been teaching my son respectful talk, mindset, and attitude for years. What about the kids who don't have diligent parents or strong mentors and role models leading them in the right direction? There isn't a solid answer for this—other than, "It takes a village." Everyone should model respectful behavior and interactions—always—so others can learn from them. If we persistently do so, workplace programs will be established, circumstances will change, and mindsets will shift.

Many men have thanked me for standing up for women in the workplace. They have daughters and fear for their future in the workplace. They don't want to see their daughters harassed or treated inappropriately. They want their daughters to be respected, to be able to perform to the best of their ability in any workplace. Some tell me their mothers or sisters have hidden devastating experiences for many years, too embarrassed or ashamed to discuss it with family, too reluctant to burden anyone else. These men are angry and feel helpless. Rightfully so. Knowing that someone you care about has suffered egregious or disrespectful behavior triggers a range of emotions. People want to fix things; to make it right. Most often, a helpful friend or family member will never be able to right that wrong, however, they can offer their support. For many women, knowing they have that support is enough to keep going.

While I continue to figure out what more support and help looks like in my world, I focus on freely giving respect through positive communication and interactions. Giving respect is free, pays dividends and creates a ripple effect of positivity and paying it forward in the lives of those it touches.

THINK ABOUT IT

- Do you feel your workplace garners respect?

- How can we be more respectful to one another?

- How can we better respond to off-script moments in life?

- Are you leading by example when it comes to respect?

- How can we perpetuate respect?

PUT IT TO WORK: TYLER IS A HARASSER

Tyler is a happily married, middle-aged man with three kids who enjoys his tenured company status. He considers himself a "lifer" at his job. He started at the company right after graduation and never looked back. If you have a good thing going, why change it? Tyler enjoys making people laugh. He likes dirty jokes and shares them frequently. Sometimes he shows new hires who is in charge through a little friendly hazing, but for the most part, Tyler does his work and provides for his family. In fact, he was the top company producer five years in a row.

Tyler often uses profanity at his workplace. He has noticed that people are more inclined to listen when he uses swear words and Tyler often needs to make a point. He wants to be taken seriously, and he usually is after he cusses out a coworker.

Tyler doesn't understand why there are so many women in his workplace. He thinks a woman's place is in the home cleaning house and raising children. It bothers Tyler that the women in his workplace ask so many questions and respond poorly to the answers they get. None of them can take a joke, either. If women want to work with men, they need to be able to handle manly talk.

One day, Tyler is called into the HR manager's office. He is told that multiple complaints have been made about his inappropriate behavior in the workplace. The HR manager lets Tyler know that his dirty jokes, inuendoes, and profanity aren't appropriate in the workplace, as is clearly reflected in their policies and mandated annual employee training.

Tyler responds with laughter and lets the HR manager know that his jokes are not offensive because everyone laughs at them.

When the HR manager confronts Tyler with a specific situation, describing detailed information and an undeniable bystander account, he proudly owns it.

As Tyler defiantly marches for the door to make his exit, the HR manager orders him to retake the online harassment training. Tyler stops, turns around, and provides one last reminder to the manager: he's helped make this company what it is today, and no amount of "stupid" training will matter at this workplace.

ASSESS THE SITUATION

- How is Tyler damaging his workplace beyond hurt feelings?

- What is missing from the conversation with Tyler and the HR manager?

- What are other ways the workplace could handle Tyler's inappropriate behavior?

- Tyler clearly does not view his behavior as inappropriate. What can be done about this?

- Can accountability be fostered with someone who does not respect others?

- What might happen if Tyler continues to harass others in this workplace or another?

CHAPTER 9

HEAL YOUR OWN WAY

> There is no singular way to recover from a job termination after facing sexual harassment, bullying, and retaliation.

Many people reach out to me and share their stories. Most are women who have experienced damaging attacks from an aggressor, and feel they experienced something like I have. The majority of these women have been fired or are close to being fired. They see the writing on the wall and want, among other things, reassurance, and advice. They all have questions, just as I did years ago, because there is no manual or guide to being fired, sexually harassed, or worse. Their questions are all similar in nature:

- Why me?
- What am I going to do now?
- How can I recover from being fired?
- How will I be able to provide for my family without this income?
- How could they do this to me?

I have never refused to speak with the targets who contact me, and I've talked to women throughout the country and from coast to coast via telephone or in person. Their stories are eerily similar. Like me, they simply want a voice and some semblance of control in an out-of-control situation. By the time I speak with them, they're at their wit's end. They've been without work for a while or have recently gotten a new job—a job that offers less pay or is nothing more than a lateral move from their previous employment. Just like me years ago, they are deeply confused and struggling to understand why they were fired and why their workplace handled things so poorly, even after they patiently worked with leadership or HR to make things right.

Some targets want to ensure their harasser does not prey upon others. While that objective may be valiant in nature, it's impossible to control. No one can control the thoughts and intentions of others. Firing a harasser will not prevent them from harassing someone else in the future.

Every time I connect with a target, I listen more than speak. It's vitally important: their voice, being heard. These women don't necessarily need to hear my pearls of wisdom or hearty pep talks assuring them that things will get better over time. They want someone to listen to their stories, to really hear them and validate their feelings. They want to connect with someone who has been through a similar experience and to find reassurance that they handled things in a proper, professional, and "right" way.

These women gave their work and workplace their all. For the most part, they enjoyed what they did and were successful by various standards. Their termination came as a shocking blow that disrupted their career trajectories. Now they simply want to make sense of a new reality. They deserve an empathetic ear, someone who can assure them that what they are feeling is valid, real, and understood. I want targets to know they aren't alone.

Unfortunately, what they experience is not an anomaly. It's a common occurrence in the modern American workplace—just as real as it was twenty-five and fifty years ago. In fact, according to a 2017 NBC News/SurveyMonkey poll, 81 percent of respondents believe sexual harassment is a problem for US businesses, yet 90 percent believe it does not occur where they work. The number of lawsuits was up 50 percent in 2018, per the US EEOC, and complaints were up by 13 percent in 2018. We can no longer deny these workplace problems.

FIND WHAT WORKS FOR YOU

After I hear targets' stories, which range from mild bullying to egregiously disgusting, the targets ask me what they should do. This is a question I cannot and should not answer—because there is no right or wrong response to this question! Sure, I can tell someone to find a lawyer or suggest therapy—and even how to go about finding the right professionals—but those approaches may not be right for them. There is no single way to recover from a job termination after facing sexual harassment, bullying, and retaliation. Self-help books are abundant, but don't be fooled; what works for one person does not work for every person. While some walk away from hurtful and traumatic experiences to focus on healing, others may not rest until they have their day in court. It's trial and error. Find the approach that works for you.

In the midst of trial and error, one step in the recovery process is essential for every target: *stop trying to figure out why you were targeted.* This is not a callous, insensitive statement. It's a realistic and protective one. I wasted a lot of time and energy ruminating over why I was targeted, verbally abused, mentally drained, and reduced to a shell of my former self. I thought knowing why I was targeted would give me closure and help me feel less sad, mad, vengeful. People want to blame something or someone for negative things that happen —to find reason in the order of things.

I lost sleep over my experience. I lost weight. I spent way too much time and energy crying buckets of tears trying to figure things out. I was fixated on receiving a public apology. I almost lost my mind over an experience I wanted to let go of all because I wanted to know *why* so very badly. I only managed to let go of *why* after realizing how far I'd travelled down a negative path. I didn't want to continue on that way, so I made a choice and flipped a switch in my mind. I shifted my perspective and stopped looking for the answer to an impossible question. Flipping the switch was the best thing I could have done.

Four realizations helped free me from the bonds of my experience. Perhaps they may help free you from yours:

1. **You will never fully figure it out.** I never understood why I was the primary target of sexual harassment and retaliation in my workplace, and I never will. I will never have the closure I originally wanted, nor will I receive a public apology. The same goes for nearly every other target. Stop wasting precious time and energy on trying to understand every aspect of what happened. Use it to love yourself a little more, search for a better job at a better organization, and re-engage with your family and friends. Again, you will never grasp the entirety of the situation, nor will you receive the answers you want or need. Get comfortable with that notion and you will feel freer.

2. **It's rarely about you.** What happened to you or any target is about the aggressor. Just like sexual harassment is never about sex; it's about power and control. The aggressor is typically someone who pushes boundaries. They may test the waters at work with dirty jokes. If left unchecked and with zero accountability, they may move on to personally attack those who squirm the most, seem the weakest, or have the most to lose—the seemingly "easy" target. You may ask, "Why me?" Because you were an easy target at the time. It isn't logical. It isn't fair, and it isn't right.

3. **Throw any preconceived notions of neat and tidy closure out the window.** Don't expect storybook justice, and don't wait for it because you may end up waiting a long time. Nothing is by the book because there is no book. Nothing will play out how you think it will.

There is little logic but many emotions linked to closure, and closure looks different for everyone. For me, it would have meant a public apology from the people who fired me. An apology was an admittance of guilt and recognition that what happened to me was real and wrong. I wanted to know they felt badly for putting me through hell. The apology never came, and it never will. It became clear during the deposition phase of my trial that the men who fired me didn't think they were in the wrong. They didn't believe they had treated me poorly or unfairly, and they didn't much care. I was simply an annoying gnat, flying in their ambitious faces, getting in the way of bigger plans.

At one deposition, my lawyer asked a senator questions about my work in relation to the workplace. He was met with evasive answers.

"And in terms of about the complaints she brought to the minority leader's office about inappropriate conduct at work, had you heard rumblings about that, too?" Mike asked.

"I hadn't heard that, but I will say that what I did hear is that… and again, that there was talk of her on…I think a better phrase is… on her way out," the senator replied.

"Do you recall who you heard that from?"

"I don't know if it was a consensus or not. I think some people had poor work experiences," the senator said. "I didn't, so when you're not really involved…my contact with Kirsten was very positive when I needed things in her role. So in that perspective …I'm sure you've learned by now senators are really focused on one person, themselves, so I really wasn't that concerned about what's going on with staffing or not. So...."

While the senator himself found nothing wrong with my work, he was more concerned about absolving himself of responsibility. The people who were in charge of managing the situation were unwilling to consider my side of it, so I knew there was no apology coming my way. I had to shift my perspective to a form of closure that would work for me.

4. **Know that one day, your pain will be less severe.** There will come a time when you don't wake up in the morning thinking about being bullied and sexually harassed, what you could or should have said, or what you would say now if you had the chance. You won't wake up in the middle of the night worrying about how you are going to make money to help your family survive. It will take time, and you won't know when it will come, but it will come. Keep on keeping on, and life will get easier day by day.

Being aware of these four truths helped my healing journey. They helped me realize how much I was getting in my own way, they gave me hope, and they drew my attention to self-awareness.

GROW SELF-AWARENESS

Becoming self-aware means recognizing why you do what you do. That includes understanding what your crutches are. You know the ones I'm talking about; the excuses you lean on to support the actions you take—or don't take—and why you do or don't take them. Your crutches justify your behavior. They might say you aren't good enough for that job, role, project, whatever. They might whisper, "That will make you uncomfortable and you don't do 'uncomfortable.'" Those crutches may help you walk but eventually, they'll also rub your under-arm raw. You'll lean to the side a bit too much to avoid the pain, changing your gait. Once you start using them, you'll be loath to give them up. Crutches can easily give you a false sense of safety.

Whatever your crutches are, they just might be helping you get in your own way. Now is the time to stop leaning on excuses. Throw your crutches away—far away—so you don't pick them up again.

When you recognize your excuses and refuse to lean on them, you'll grow stronger. You'll begin to recognize other aspects of your perspective and behaviors, and then you have a choice: you can change your behavior if you don't like something. Test an option. Relish the fact you have the opportunity to choose. If one decision doesn't work for you, take another look at those crutches—the excuses you're making—and make another choice. Move on.

The power of choice galvanized me. It helped me regain my self-confidence and control over my thoughts, actions, and life. I didn't embrace it until I came to a fork in the road. It was tiring getting out of bed in the morning. My first thoughts of the day focused on negativity. I was so depressed about being fired because I tried to do what was right that I wallowed in misery and suspicion. My thoughts were out of control and caught in a negative loop. The unhealthy mindset exhausted me. I realized I had to find a way to be happier or the negativity would consume me. I had to make a choice. Did I want bitterness, resentment, and revenge to consume my day, or did I want something better?

I chose to be happy. Once I made that choice, I stuck by it. Every time a negative, self-denigrating thought crossed my mind, I stopped and asked myself, "What is the opposite of that thought?" I would repeat the opposite, more positive thought over and over until it took root and grew.

KEEPING IT REAL

Thanks to social media and our society focused on instant gratification, I see way too much judgement about others' choices. In this online, digitally connected world, we constantly see in real time what people are thinking, feeling, and doing—whether we like it or not. Social media has become a fake reality where people lean on trivialities to hide their true selves. Are duck lips, doe eyes, and the fact that someone volunteered at the local food bank for ten hours a true reflection of who they are? Possibly, but people are only leaning on what they view as exemplary qualities or circumstances as an excuse for their perceived shortcomings. They post what they think you want to know or see. It's a one-sided, superficial projection of reality. An "easy" form of communication because it avoids the hard stuff. It leans on crutches instead of considering the full weight of life's complications and realities. Sharing a weight loss journey is more than pictures of what you make for a meal. And the photographer of those fun pictures of cats wearing clothes is surely covered in scratches. Reality is messy, complicated, and not always fun. For the most part, we do not see those aspects of life on social media feeds.

Getting rid of crutches and confronting reality after being traumatized is a process. As a work in progress, I still grab my crutches from time to time. Then I trip over them. My crutches got in the way a few years ago when my husband and I got into a fight. We were sitting in a pizza restaurant in Geneva, Wisconsin on a cold, rainy fall evening and wishing we were in our own home under a blanket. We had just left the Alpine Valley music venue after standing in the rain for the annual Farm Aid concert. We were soaked, tired, and feeling queasy from all the cigarette smoke allowed in the venue. To make things worse, we left before the headliners took the stage because we could not endure the elements anymore. Eating pizza in a dark restaurant instead of listening to our favorite bands was frustrating; more so because we were both tired and burned out, and neither one of us wanted to say it to the other because we were too focused on pleasing one another. We invested a good amount of money into a weekend concert adventure that was supposed to be fun.

"I know how much this weekend meant to you," I said.

"I thought this weekend meant a lot to *you!*" Jeff replied. "I didn't want to come here. Are you crazy? Stop trying to make me happy. You have to stop your people-pleasing."

And then it hit me. I had turned most of my decisions into people-pleasing. That was my crutch. If I did what everyone else wanted, there was no risk of conflict. And I didn't want any more conflict in my life. Unfortunately, refusing to engage in any sort of debate over decisions with my husband unfairly burdened him with responsibility for everything from entertainment options to parenting and meal selection: "Whatever you'd like to eat, dear."

The Wisconsin incident made me realize that I'm lucky to be married to someone who is my equal partner in marriage and in every way. We began our lives together in a true collaboration, sharing duties and decisions from cooking and cleaning to parenting and discipline. Falling into a pattern of "people-pleasing" my own husband and using him as a crutch was a sad state of affairs.

We all have issues. We all face tough situations and encounter questionable scenarios. We all struggle with something that others know nothing about. Remember this: there is always someone out there who *wants* to know about it. Someone who wants to understand it—and you. You aren't alone, and you were never meant to be alone. Being real and forthcoming others will open a whole new world to you.

Excuses are barriers to better things. Once you put down your excuses, do what needs to be done to make better things happen. Put up Post-It Notes with positive self-affirmations. Send yourself a letter of encouragement. Keep a journal, meet with a therapist, or join a support group—do what you need to do to eliminate your crutches in an effort to open your mind to betterment. You deserve it and will feel:

FREE AT LAST

Although I experienced a certain euphoria when the verdict was announced at my trial, it took almost five years to fully break free from the chains of my situation, to feel less fearful and sad, less suspicious, lighter. During every job interview after my termination, I prayed the interviewer would not ask anything about my previous employment.

For far too long after I finally got a new job, I was suspicious that my work was being highly scrutinized, just as it had been at the Iowa Legislature. I live in a relatively small community where everyone knows a friend of a friend. Because my termination had been highly publicized, I was fearful my new coworkers would press me about my previous horrible experience, or worse yet, talk politics and make me into a villain for attempting to hold my former employer accountable.

My son started preschool in the fall of 2013, right after I was fired, and I desperately did not want the other parents to find out about my situation or that I was local headline news for so long. I felt shame that I was fired. Shame that there were people out there saying I did bad work or that I couldn't hold a job. Those fearful thoughts seem ridiculous now, but I had been reduced to a state of constant fear. No one should live there. Don't let anyone banish you to that place, including yourself.

I've learned to let things go a bit more. I've learned to care less about what people think of me and my work because I have grown in confidence and skill. There are only a select few people in this world whom I care about. They tell me when my work that is merely okay, or when I'm being dramatic or unreasonable. They keep me in check. They are all that matter.

THINK ABOUT IT

- Recognize what matters most to you and focus on it.

- Identify your crutches and how they make you comfortable.

- Throw your crutches out a window, bury them, do what it takes to get rid of them.

- You will survive moments of being uncomfortable.

- Connect in the real world with others and don't judge their choices.

- Excuses are barriers to betterment. Be open to the possibility of betterment in your life and know that you deserve it.

- You can choose happiness.

PUT IT TO WORK:
SHAWNDA WORRIES BEYOND WORK

Shawnda has worked at her small town's gas station and convenient store for twenty-five years and is a happy, positive presence in the community. She welcomes each guest as they enter the store and is ready to take on any job from shoveling the sidewalks when it snows to running the cash register and cleaning the bathroom.

Shawnda has a new coworker, Robert. Shawnda has known Robert for years because he is the son of the pastor at Shawnda's church, the bedrock of the small community. A lifelong member of the congregation, she attends church weekly and is a fixture at most events. Her church family, which includes all her friends, is important to her. When Shawnda and her friends are not at church, they are in each other's homes playing cards, sharing meals, or making blankets for the church's missions project. Shawnda knows she would be lost without them.

Robert is also active in the church community. He takes part in many activities and fundraisers and is well-liked by all parishioners. Unfortunately, Robert is not a great coworker. He pays more attention to Shawnda than to the tasks he is supposed to complete.

At first, Shawnda cuts Robert some slack and helps him with his work. After a few weeks, his attention to Shawnda grows more intense. He leans in close to Shawnda, ogling her and making suggestive comments about her appearance. Shawnda tries to divert Robert's by his attention with gentle rebuttals and giving him more tasks to do, but none of her approaches work. Instead, they seem to intensify Robert's interest.

Shawnda ignores him until his comments become overtly sexual in nature. Finally, Shawnda talks to her manager, who attends the same church, about changing schedules. When the manager asks Shawnda why she is requesting the shift change, Shawnda confesses that Robert's inappropriate behavior is an issue, and she no longer feels comfortable working with him.

Shawnda assumes the conversation she had with her manager was private and confidential, but the next day, Robert is angry and even more aggressive toward Shawnda. Shortly after they begin working separate shifts, Robert shows up when Shawnda is on duty. He leans over the counter, red-faced and hisses in Shawnda's ear that she shouldn't try to get away from him. That they work best together in more ways than one. When another staff person quits, the manager has no choice but to put Shawnda and Robert together on the same shift again from time to time. Roger is still angry with her, and his aggressive behavior intensifies. Shawnda grows more scared and worried. She is afraid to trust her manager again, and she does not dare turn to her church family for support. They all know Robert and see him as an upstanding churchgoer like his pastor father. Shawnda has witnessed her social circle criticize and push out parishioners for smaller things.

Because the town is so small, there are few other jobs. Shawnda fears losing all she holds dear by pursuing the issue further. She also fears for her safety by continuing to work with Robert at the convenience store. She can't yet prove anything, but she suspects Robert is sabotaging Shawnda's work at the store to make her look bad.

ASSESS THE SITUATION

- What can Shawnda do to feel safe?

- How can Robert be such a great member of the church and such a bad coworker?

- Was there any other way Shawnda could have handled her interactions with Robert?

- How can Shawnda deal with her fears of being ostracized?

- How can Shawnda reach out to her church family support system?

CHAPTER 10

THE ROAD TO FORGIVENESS

> I have yet to meet a target who has forgiven their harasser.
> Their journeys have been just as long as mine and no less
> unique. I also have yet to meet a harasser who exhibits remorse
> or apologizes for their misdeeds.

FORGIVENESS CAN CREATE healing, and it can be transformative.
It can provide peace and solace after anguish and chaos. It stirs growth,
self-awareness, and increased self-confidence. But forgiveness is also
complex and not everyone is ready for it. It cannot be forced.

I envy those who are ready to forgive, who make letting go of in-
justice look easy. I still wrestle with forgiveness. Bitter and resentful at
times, I finally settled on the idea that forgiveness is a journey, a road I'm
traveling down. Many checkpoints appear along the path, and I don't
know when I'll reach my destination, but I'm optimistic I'll eventually
arrive.

The act of forgiveness has its own timeline and demands. For some,
it may mean simply moving on or wiping the slate clean. For others, it
may mean waiting years on end for a heartfelt apology. Some people
have mapped out steps to forgiveness. Others, like me, struggle with it
for years. I beat myself up over coulda-woulda-shoulda moments; the

worry that I possibly didn't do enough, didn't respond well enough to the harassment I suffered. I yearn for forgiveness to fall neatly into place so I can move on.

FORGIVE YOURSELF

It's particularly hard to forgive someone else if you're harboring judgement against yourself. How can you let someone else off the hook if you're still on it? Extending forgiveness to yourself opens a doorway to relief. According to Professor Prakash Gangdev in the online Indian Journal of Psychiatry, "Self-forgiveness is the willingness to abandon self-resentment in the face of one's own acknowledged objective wrong, while fostering compassion, generosity, and love toward oneself."[21]

Forgiving my oppressors wasn't even in my peripheral view immediately after I was fired. I had more pressing matters to attend to. My only concern was how I would pay all our family bills in two weeks. Once I calmed my fears, re-budgeted family finances, and started an open dialogue with my husband about everything we faced, I was able to think about things like healing my own self-doubts and lack of confidence, and ultimately, my journey to forgiveness.

I began to realize how badly stress was affecting my mental state, and that impacted everything. It made me tired of life. Reducing mental and physical exhaustion to a manageable level helped me cope. It gave me space to handle other things like finding work and self-care. Self-care is imperative. If you're mentally exhausted, gift yourself with rest. Even five minutes of meditation or being alone, sans devices, makes a difference. When your brain rests, your body will follow.

As my mind cleared, I began to understand that I didn't truly love myself. I wasn't compassionate or generous toward myself or my recovery. Self-forgiveness became a new focus. I managed to let some things go such as worrying about what people thought about me. When I was able to do that, other problems shrank in comparison and eventually lost importance.

Researchers trying to pin down the benefits of forgiveness say there's "therapeutic potential" in forgiveness. They liken it to a release of vengeance and bitterness toward the perpetrator of an offense.[22] Call it what you will, the fact that forgiveness heals the soul is undeniable: studies have shown that forgiveness affects mental health outcomes, and it plays a role in how depression and anxiety play out. It also plays a role in physical health outcomes. The act of forgiveness has been linked to cardiovascular and nervous system health, lower cholesterol, and reduced risk of heart attack. By releasing the psychological and physiological toll of trauma, forgiveness puts power back into the hands of someone who has suffered abuse.

MY OWN FORGIVENESS JOURNEY

Forgiveness comes relatively easily when you're dealing with honest mistakes or people who apologize for their occasional misdeeds. Forgiveness grows stickier with heavier transgressions like murder, adultery, harassment, and predatory behavior. How to respond differs for every individual. Forgiveness is such a unique journey that we can't assume others are ready to freely dole it out or even talk about it. Never tell someone to forgive the person who caused them harm. It's terrible advice that will only create hurt feelings and angst. A better approach might be to ask how they feel about forgiveness and how you can support them.

For someone who is deeply traumatized, forgiveness requires a huge shift in perspective. Unless the perpetrator has extended remorse, forgiveness can feel very one-sided. It's hard to forgive someone who seems oblivious to the harm they caused. Targets want to see remorse. They want validation and reassurance that what happened to them won't happen to someone else.

It's worth noting that either consciously or subconsciously, some people view exacting revenge as a doorway to forgiveness. Harboring notions of revenge feels cathartic and purposeful, even though it's self-destructive and emotionally damaging. Finding a way to release anger may be more healing in the long run.

I think a lot about remorse, accountability, and empathy as precursors to forgiveness because I didn't receive any from my workplace. If my harassers had expressed regret for their behavior, I would have been less vengeful, more forgiving. I probably wouldn't have pursued retribution so forcefully. A simple, "I'm sorry for what you experienced," would have changed everything.

"You're not the same person I married," Jeff told me during a crucial conversation about exiting my toxic work environment. "And I don't like what your workplace has done to you. To us."

Jeff's words cut deep, but I knew he was right. I didn't like who I had become either. After being repeatedly torn down, I was negative, suspicious, and constantly on edge. My husband helped me realize that being the butt of so many jokes wasn't normal. Going along was not a productive response to the situation. Going along wouldn't get my confidence back. Going along wouldn't change my environment for the better.

When I finally decided to stand up for myself, I got people's attention. Standing up made me feel strong and helped me regain self-confidence. It opened the door to self-forgiveness, something I needed to find before I could forgive anyone else. As my confidence returned and I grew stronger, I did manage to find moments of satisfaction.

After I was fired, the senate minority leader continued to ignore and dismiss the toxic work environment at the Iowa Statehouse. In mid-November 2017,[23] a few months after my court appearance, he held a rather painful press conference where he changed his tune and said he believed my testimony. This was several years after I had been fired, so it didn't have quite the same impact it would have had if he'd apologized earlier.

Presumably, political pressure helped him determine that an investigation of the work environment should take place and that an HR person needed to be hired.

Not long ago, I visited the Iowa Statehouse to shadow a legislator in the House of Representatives. The visit was related to a program I was involved with that trained Democrat women to run for office. Walking into the building rattled my nerves. I knew I'd bump into people from my past who didn't support or respect me. I also knew I had to get over my fear and go inside anyway. I had to stop caring so much about their opinions of me.

Ultimately, the day went well. A legislator I had previously worked for greeted me with genuine warmth. He asked how my family was doing and spent more than a cordial amount of time in a conversation that reached beyond pleasantries. The conversation was a nice surprise as this man had greatly disappointed me with his silence when I was terminated. He admitted that he'd been assured that the staff problem—me—was "being taken care of." Because "taken care of" implied finality, my senator friend did nothing. He asked no clarifying questions, offered no gestures of kindness, and didn't check on staff wellbeing or morale. He took the easy way out.

In that moment, I realized it wasn't worth my time to harbor ill will or bitterness toward someone like him. A person who was overtly friendly toward me in a crowded public place but would look the other way in private was more concerned about how others perceived them than they were about me. They likely wouldn't appreciate my forgiveness, even if I offered it.

I'm baffled and disappointed that an entire caucus of twenty-four legislators avoided addressing a highly controversial and contentious situation that was all over the local news. Such complacency is especially disappointing from elected officials who are—or should be—held to a higher standard. I wasted a lot of time being angry at these people and wanting to exact some sort of revenge—even though I realized revenge would never change them or make them feel remorseful. It would never truly bring me joy, either. Thoughts of retribution stole my energy, making me negative and spiteful. I didn't want to expose my son to those qualities so a part of me let go and moved on.

Only one person I worked for reached out with a phone call after I was terminated: a senator who had previously served as minority leader. We had shared a good professional relationship, and he was always respectful and honest. He made a point to find out how I was doing personally, and that meant the world to me. The brief conversation made me feel valued. His kindness provided a dose of gratitude and hope in human good nature and offered a stark contrast to the silence I received from those who caused me pain.

IN LIEU OF APOLOGIES

I have yet to meet a target who has forgiven their harasser. Their journeys have been just as long as mine and no less unique. I also have yet to meet a harasser who exhibits remorse or apologizes for their misdeeds. These two factors are inextricably linked. If a harasser doesn't apologize—I mean really apologize—by saying the words, "I'm sorry for the pain I caused you," the target's pain will usually continue until they find a way to relieve it themselves. Not an easy task.

High-profile aggressors often dance around apologies by saying things like, "If I would have known," or "It's unfortunate she feels that way," without taking ownership or responsibility for their actions. They are too focused on self-preservation.

Thanks to the #MeToo movement, more people are aware of sexual harassment as an insidious, pervasive problem. As we continue to publicly call out bullying and inappropriate behavior, we hold perpetrators' feet to the fire. Society is finally beginning to examine inequality at various levels. This reckoning is a great leap forward for many targets. Knowing that others recognize their plight may compensate for the lack of apologies from perpetrators.

I do a lot of praying and the act of forgiveness finds its way into my prayers. But this journey is hard, and all I can do is take one step at a time. I've become more aware of others' inability to support struggling coworkers or simply express regret. While this used to enrage me, it no longer does. Most people aren't born to empathize with and nurture others. These are learned abilities, not innate concepts. Until empathy becomes more common, targets may need to find paths to forgiveness in lieu of apologies.

I used to facilitate training for engaging in crucial conversations at a technology company. Sensitive discussions were often avoided because of fear. Fear of awkwardness, fear of damaging a relationship, fear of ruining a project. Feeling a little awkward will pass as the conversation gets going. All of these fears are manageable if empathy comes to the table. A solid relationship will withstand uncomfortable conversations out of mutual respect. If a project is ruined because participants ventured into uncomfortable conversational territory, there are probably bigger issues at hand.

We need to face our fears and engage in crucial conversations. Ask for or offer support rather than complacency. Talk about what help and support means and what it can look like in workplaces and personal lives. More than just our workplaces will change if we step away from complacency and start doing something about harassment and bullying.

As we travel our unique roads, we must remember to never push anyone toward forgiveness. Forgiveness is not mandatory, and it may not be the right choice for everyone.

THINK ABOUT IT

- The road to forgiveness is a different journey for everyone. Respect that.

- Self-forgiveness is an important part of the overall healing journey.

- Practice self-care regularly and rest any way you can. Self-care helps with healing.

- Harassers won't always apologize. In lieu of an apology or a show of remorse that might prompt forgiveness, targets still need to move beyond their experience. What that means will vary from target to target.

- Learning, practicing, and executing crucial conversations with others is the opposite of complacency.

PUT IT TO WORK: JODY WANTS FORGIVENESS

Jody is her boss' favorite employee and can get away with just about any kind of behavior. To retain that favor, she aggressively pursues deadlines and pushes her subordinates at every turn with no regard for their personal circumstances. She justifies her actions when they complain and tells them that hard work builds character.

When Anya begins working in Jody's department, issues immediately arise. Anya seems nervous and uncertain. Her work is not completed to Jody's standards. From time to time, Anya arrives late to work and meetings. These red flags catch the eye of Jody's boss, who insists Jody help Anya along to boost department productivity and numbers. As Jody helps Anya, she begins to see Anya's talent for the job. Anya increasingly contributes to the quality of the department's work. Jody's boss is so impressed with Anya that Jody feels her status is in jeopardy. Anya becomes a target.

No behavior is off limits to Jody. She criticizes or yells at Anya for everything from being one minute late or wearing the wrong color in her company ID photo to choosing the wrong makeup. Jody even lectures Anya on the importance of who she sits with for lunch in the company cafeteria. Jody bullies and micromanages Anya to the point of exhaustion. One morning, Anya does not come into work. Jody flies into a rage. After spewing unkind remarks throughout the department about her coworker, Jody discovers that a severe anxiety attack sent Anya to the hospital. Anya never returns to work, and the boss blames Jody for the loss of an outstanding employee who will be expensive to replace.

The tables are turned. Jody is no longer the boss' favorite. Jody is highly scrutinized, micromanaged, and picked apart by her boss, who makes it difficult for Jody to do her job. When Jody misses a simple project deadline, she is fired.

The loss of her work identity sends Jody into a tailspin and a deep self-analysis. Ultimately, she seeks counseling and begins to understand how her treatment of others was harsh, overblown, and unnecessary. When she realizes the best way forward means making amends with the people she bullied, Jody emails Anya and asks if she can call and apologize to her.

It takes Anya months to return Jody's email. Ultimately, Anya agrees to a phone call. Eager to obtain forgiveness and be let off the hook, Jody demands Anya accept her apology.

ASSESS THE SITUATION

- What do you think Jody is feeling?

- Why is Jody *demanding* Anya accept her apology?

- How else could Jody have handled her apology to Anya?

- How could Jody express true remorse and empathy?

- What questions might Jody ask of Anya if she were truly concerned about Anya's wellbeing?

- How might the situation be different if Jody had not experienced bullying and retaliation herself?

CHAPTER 11

FROM JUDGEMENT DAY TO NORMALCY

> A new door had opened. For the first time in a long time, I felt no worry, fear, or shame. I just felt happy. And I felt compelled to use my experience to help others.

I WOKE UP on Tuesday, July 18, 2017 prickling with pins and needles of dread and anticipation. It seemed like any other summer morning, but it could be life-changing for me. Any day now, the jury could reach a judgement on my harassment suit against the State of Iowa. After checking the weather forecast. I made sure my seven-year-old son was up, fed, and getting ready for day camp. I said my morning prayer, dressed for the hot day ahead, and headed off to work as a communication consultant with an employer who seemed to appreciate my efforts.

I had nervous energy to spare. I had spent the previous week on a roller coaster of emotions in the most stressful setting of my entire life—the courtroom—witnessing the culmination of four years of legal work.

Mike had easily proven sexual harassment, but I was nervous about the wrongful termination and retaliation portion of the suit. They would be tougher points for a jury to agree upon.

Enduring a trial is an experience of seclusion for everyone involved. As a plaintiff, you are advised to not discuss anything with anyone but your lawyer. Trials takes place during business hours, so you aren't able to go to work either. Witnesses called to testify aren't permitted to watch or read the news until after they finish giving their testimony. The same thing goes for jurors. They can't speak out or reach out because outside influence could taint their judgement.

I had survived the full week of my trial with little food, too nervous to be hungry, and I endured late hours with my lawyer pouring over lines of questioning and practicing my answers for the moment I took the stand.

Early afternoon on Tuesday the 18th, my lawyer called and told me to find a private place in my office building where we could talk. I went to the closest and most quiet area I could find: the elevator bank.

"We won," Mike said energetically. "On all three counts—wrongful termination, sexual harassment, and retaliation!"

"What did you say?" I blurted out.

"We won."

I burst into tears.

"The jury has also awarded you an amount," Mike continued as I softly cried.

I wiped my eyes. "Oh? What is it?" I had nearly forgotten about the monetary aspect of things. The fact that I had won was still sinking in.

"Kirsten, they awarded you 2.2 million dollars," Mike replied calmly.

I was shocked at the amount, something we hadn't asked for. Mike explained that the jury decided to award that sum based upon everything revealed at trial. Our four-year legal battle was finally over. Mike's phone call triggered a tidal wave of emotions. As I stood in front of the elevator crying with relief and exhilaration, a coworker walked by. She asked if everything was okay. It was more than okay, I told her. The verdict confirmed in a very public way the fact that I had been sexually harassed, retaliated against, and then wrongfully terminated after giving five years of my life to an abusive workplace. My coworker and the elected officials who created our state laws abused their privileges of power and neglected the very laws they made, and we had proven it beyond a reasonable doubt. A few hours later, we met at the Polk County courthouse and offered a statement to local media outlets.

Numerous things happened on Judgement Day. My self-worth and professional reputation were renewed, but there was something else, too. I had a tugging sense that I could not simply take this win, go home, and gloat. I felt compelled to channel my hard-fought win and renewed self-confidence into advocacy. I had to share my story with the world and use it to support and educate others. A mission was born to untangle the complexities surrounding a subject that has remained in the shadows and whispers around water coolers for far too long.

I survived harassment, degradation, crippling self-doubt. I survived televised testimony in a court of law and sharing deeply personal revelations in front of strangers. I lived to tell the tale and accomplished something most people are unable or unwilling to do; I held my harassers accountable. I spoke out, and I was victorious. If I could do it, others could impart accountability, survive, and thrive, too.

We weren't completely out of the woods yet, however. Mike had warned me earlier that the State could appeal the jury's decision. They typically appealed cases to protect their money but doing so would create another long and potentially drawn-out court battle lasting several more years. I knew about drawn-out court battles. Just getting my case into the courtroom to begin with required months waiting for appearance scheduling. Months more waiting for Appellate judges to rule on whether to allow the case to go forward or not. It was agonizing. I didn't want to go through that again or put my family and former coworkers through it.

Luckily, the State didn't want to go back to court either. We reached an agreement minutes before the deadline to make an appeal. Immense relief filled my soul after I shook hands with the Iowa's solicitor general, who was the top acting attorney general on my case. His handshake represented the word of the state: we would never have to return to court on the issue of me being sexually harassed, retaliated against, and wrongfully terminated. A book I had never wanted to open had finally closed.

After the handshake, the judge was notified of our agreement. As both parties and our lawyers left the courthouse, the press that had hounded me for so long simply scattered. The story was over. We all walked back to our normal, everyday lives.

But life did not feel normal to me. A new door had opened. For the first time in a long time, I felt no worry, fear, or shame. I just felt happy.

FINDING (NEW) NORMALCY

Normalcy is different for everyone. For me, what it means has changed. Before I was fired, "normal" was a constant state of questioning. *Who will say something embarrassing to me today? Can I make it through the day without crying? How can I fight back without pushing the envelope far enough to lose my job?* While ridiculous at face value, those thoughts occurred daily in my old job. I felt I had to be constantly ready for blows of harassment and retaliation. I didn't know where they'd come from or how hard they'd be thrown.

After being fired, normalcy shifted. I was suspicious of everyone and everything—not a great way to carry on in life. I was still prepared for blows, although for different reasons. I constantly felt as though others were judging me. The fact that my firing was being disputed in the court of public opinion was tough. The black mark of employment termination on my record left me feeling ashamed, regardless of how it got there. Those perspectives seriously harmed any sense of accomplishment I garnered, and after years of mental abuse, my level of self-doubt was high.

Embarrassment and suspicion not only made it challenging to find a new job, but tougher on my life in general. I very much needed a paycheck in order for my family to make ends meet. I needed support and strong positive relationships in my life to feel like a regular human again. I also very much relied on anti-depressants and counseling. Embarrassment and suspicion hung around me like a fog that took time to clear.

I applied to so many jobs in the summer after I was fired that I lost count. I attended twelve interviews in the span of three months. Every day I checked countless websites and created accounts with local employment groups. Interviewers were always kind. Some of them clearly tiptoed around sensitive questions in the interview process. I could tell they had done their research on me, and I thought long and hard about how I answered their questions during the interview process. I didn't want any employer to think I was a troublemaker or that I was on a crusade to "out" each and every inappropriate person and action at a workplace. I simply wanted a job so I could pay my bills.

I got good at responding without revealing too much. "I would appreciate it if you didn't contact my previous employer as we didn't see eye-to-eye," or "We had a difference of opinion and I'm no longer there." The understatement of the century! I distinctly remember almost choking over that last phrase. It took everything in me to hold back the rage bubbling up in my throat. Ultimately, employers passed me over for several jobs I was qualified for, and maybe even some that I was over-qualified for, due to my high-profile situation. I had picked a fight with Goliath, so what did I expect? For many employers, a giant fighter is too much to take on in an employee.

I finally found employment in the fall of 2013, thanks to my husband. He had gone to his employer and mentioned that we might need to move. The high-profile nature of my court case was making it tough for me to find work. My husband's employer valued him as an outstanding person and employee, and they knew that the happiness and stability of our family would help him. Ultimately, that would help them and their bottom line. So they took me on. I spent the next three years working for them in a variety of positions from marketing to HR and tried to carve out a niche in the training and professional development area. I bounced around a lot trying to redirect my professional skills.

The experience allowed me to pick up the pieces of my life and melt back into anonymity. I had regularity, directives, projects, and deadlines, and coworkers and bosses who didn't talk down to me, berate, harass, or bully me. No one asked me questions about my case or my experience, and I was able to re-establish my personal value connected to work. Some people depended on me and that was a great feeling—to be valued. My contribution to this organization was recognized. My job impacted others in a positive way, and they told me so. It was something I hadn't felt in a long time. I believe everyone should find a place or an environment where they can experience that feeling, because it matters a great deal to a person. It encourages engagement and loyalty to an organization and simply makes a better employee.

I'm so grateful for that job and the opportunities it provided to learn new things and work amongst amazing people I would not have otherwise interacted with.

If you have not had that kind of experience, I urge you to find it. Search and experiment until you find a place where you are valued. The feeling of being valued is hard to replicate and it's bankable. It's normalcy. When employees feel needed, they will continue to work to attain and pass on that feeling to others. The employee pays it forward in dividends of various types. Others see it and strive for it and it spreads like wildfire.

COMFORT AND CONFIDENCE

Now that I recognize the difference between a healthy and an unhealthy workplace and the impacts of each, my expectations are tempered and realistic. When I visit workplaces, I take a hard look at their culture and what type of atmosphere employers and employees are trying to create. At most organizations, it's easy to spot what's wrong fairly quickly. It's either a culture of comfort and confidence, or it isn't. Comfort and confidence are things every workplace needs and benefits from. The concept is simple and free for anyone who will listen and work for it.

An organization with a culture of comfort and confidence creates psychological safety. Workers are free, empowered to take risk, and they more openly share ideas that could benefit the company. The opposite culture creates fear and intimidation, which stifles creativity. It poisons the environment and everyone in it.

Think about the great places you have worked, have read about, or observed from a distance. They have a thriving culture of comfort and confidence. Accountability is key. Upper management regularly interacts with staff. Relationships are formed. Workers within these organizations hold each other up and root for each other's success through cohesive teamwork that benefits the organization's bottom line. And they get stuff done.

Everyone loves to get stuff done! That feeling of accomplishment and cohesiveness is second to none. Even if you simply like to punch the clock, come in to work with your head down, and not interact with another soul, you like to get stuff done. Believe it or not, some organizations don't provide employees with what they need to achieve comfort and confidence, and that prevents them from getting stuff done.

Questions to ask when assessing workplace culture:

1. Are my coworkers and I free to share our ideas without being ridiculed, chastised or worse?

2. Do my coworkers and I have regular check ins with organizational leadership and management?

3. Is employee feedback regularly sought regarding company policies, processes, and practices?

4. Is accountability regularly reinforced?

5. Can I have a frank, honest discussion with my colleagues at my workplace without fear of retaliation?

6. Am I valued and does my work matter?

7. Do my colleagues and I feel comfortable calling out and reporting inappropriate behavior?

8. Do I go to and leave work feeling good about my job and the work I'm doing?

Did you notice that some of these questions have an emotional component to them? Being valued in a work setting elicits joy, happiness, empathy, and respect, which leads to engagement, productivity, and a feeling of safety.

Of course, a slew of negative feelings arises when the concept of a comfort and confidence culture is not effectively practiced. This can result in a highly charged, volatile environment. I lived through the negative thoughts and feelings associated with a toxic culture. They are tough to grapple with or even understand if they aren't recognized. Often people causing damage may be mere symptoms of the toxic environment.

Toxic workplaces are common and occur when inappropriate behavior is severe and pervasive. The environment perpetuates because those in charge are ill-equipped to make change, don't want or care to make change, or benefit from the toxicity in some way. To be blunt, the leaders and workers in these workplaces don't value or respect one another. They have their heads in the sand and will only learn the hard way that change must come.

THINK ABOUT IT:

- "Normal" is a relative term. Normalcy is different for everyone.

- Normalcy is what targets seek, contrary to the thought that money solves problems.

- Doing the right thing is not easy, however, it's worthwhile.

- Workplace culture is important and valuable, and everyone deserves to experience an environment of comfort and confidence.

PUT IT TO WORK:
MARY WANTS TO WORK

Mary is an enthusiastic fighter for women's rights. Her fight began after she was wrongfully terminated from her job as a receptionist in a local dentist's office. The dentist who owned the business kept pressuring her for sex. He made her promises and bought her gifts. Being attracted to him and knowing they were two single consenting adults, she finally relented. Then she was fired.

When Mary threatened to take the dentist to court, the two parties ultimately came to a settlement with a monetary sum and a nondisclosure agreement. The settlement Mary agreed to is enough to support her for a year while she looks for other employment.

Mary attends every women's rights rally, club meeting, and protest she can. She loves the adrenaline rush she gets from being surrounded by others who have experienced something similar to her and she finds activism to be a constructive way to redirect her anger. She makes signs, speaks passionately through a bullhorn, and rouses any crowd she encounters. She knows her enthusiasm shows others they can fight for something too. She knows people listen, and she wants to be heard.

Unfortunately, Mary is having trouble getting a job. Her nondisclosure agreement ensures she cannot talk about her last employer or why she was fired. Most job application forms ask why she left her previous employment. Mary knows that how she fills out that form will determine whether she gets a call for an interview. Mary also knows that her advocacy might interfere with her ability to find employment. During one recent interview, she was recognized from nightly news coverage of recent protests. As Mary attempted to discuss her advocacy work further with the interviewer, the interviewer made clear that "those kinds" of protests were not supported at that workplace. Mary knew she would not get the job.

ASSESS THE SITUATION

- What judgements did you make about Mary?

- Mary's career trajectory has been interrupted; how can she continue to find gainful employment? How could her support system help?

- How has Mary's new advocacy community affected her?

- Should advocacy and a workplace be exclusive? Why or why not?

- What emotions do you think Mary is wrestling with?

- Why do you think Mary agreed to a settlement and nondisclosure agreement?

CHAPTER 12
WHAT NOW?

What you say and do matters. It can change the world!

OUR WORLD IS complex, our realities diverse and challenging. Unpacking next steps for any healing journey may feel overwhelming or even useless in a world where confusion and misinformation are prevalent, and bullies are world leaders. There is more to the issue of workplace harassment than simply wanting it to end and hoping people become nicer. That's a helplessness mentality. Instead, we must take action, live out healthy responses to harassment in word and deed, and empower others to do the same.

This book illustrates how far from helpless you are. Use what you've discovered in these pages to smash misconceptions to bits, change the vernacular to enable healthy dialogue, and discount any preconceived notions that may be holding you down or back. It's okay to not be okay sometimes. It's okay to voice concerns about workplace environments and question status quo. It's certainly okay to stand up for what is right and actively engage in building workplaces that reduce fear, shame, and guilt. When we work together to make change, we all win. We increase the momentum behind change with a powerful force called advocacy.

ADVOCACY

The goal of advocacy is to influence decisions. As an advocate for safe and healthy workplaces, I engage in educational processes rather than confrontation. I help others understand a complex issue that affects people all over the world. I address groups of people, but I work behind the scenes with lawmakers too. We seek legislation to create better environments for workers and to infuse accountability in ways that help, rather than harm, targets. As someone who used to work on the front end with legislators, I realize there are times when it's more valuable to let others take the lead. My efforts are focused not on me, but on creating positive change in an area that desperately needs it.

Advocacy isn't just good for others; it's good for you too. Becoming an advocate helped renew my confidence and rediscover my voice. I'm using both to influence decisions that will improve conditions for everyone, for every workplace. Promoting safer, harassment-free workplaces is about empowerment—for me and others. Initially, my engagement with advocacy may have been totally self-serving, however, I quickly discovered that sharing my experiences supported a better, farther-reaching practice. Teaching employers and workers best practices for combatting harassment made me feel I had something to offer that helps everyone.

Advocacy is what you make of it. Lawyers often serve as advocates, and they are paid for their support, but one does not require a juris doctorate to become an advocate. Passion and purpose will do.

LEARNING TO ADVOCATE

There are several levels of advocacy: self, peer, group, professional, to name a few. Whether male or female, you may already be involved with grassroots work and not even realize it; you remind your boss about the impact of your last project and share statistics to back it up, or you speak with your team about the positive effects resulting from the last year of working together.

It may be time to move your informal efforts into a more formal advocate process:

1. **Be intentional.** Say "no" more often. "No" is particularly hard for women to say for a variety of reasons. Remember that saying "no" to a request or activity shouldn't stir regret. Rather, view it as an opportunity to look out for yourself and preserve your precious time and energy. When you say "no" to a type of advocacy you are only remotely passionate about, you have more room for what you are truly passionate about.

2. **Fight for what is right for you.** You know what truly matters in your life, and you know the reasons you do what you do. Always keep that in mind when making decisions. Never waver.

3. **Work to educate others.** Those around you should realize your worth and the weight of your contributions. If they don't, enlighten them about the important things you are doing, why you are doing them, and how you are an integral member of the team. It's not bragging; it's a fact and you have the information to back it up.

4. **Engage in outreach.** Make an effort to step outside your comfort zone. Accept opportunities you usually wouldn't tackle. Reach out to people you wouldn't usually talk to. Don't let fear get in the way. You'll be more self-aware and better able to stretch your limits. You'll also learn more about yourself in the process.

Advocating more for yourself isn't as difficult as it sounds, and it's extremely rewarding. You won't regret it because advocating means using your voice. It helps develop confidence and strength. That's powerful.

After years of practice, I no longer have qualms about sharing some parts of my personal life before an audience of hundreds. Speaking to large groups gives me a rush of adrenaline. My connection with the crowd grows as I share my story, and their energy fuels me to keep going. My story, like everyone else's, has elements that we can all relate to. That helps me easily find common ground with almost anyone I encounter. I have many opportunities to create a sense of shared purpose. This helps keep hope alive in my heart and guides me on my mission to end workplace harassment. I want to educate others on the wrongs I encountered so that "rights" can be passed on, hurt feelings and high-strung emotions avoided. I don't want what happened to me to happen to anyone else.

Although it isn't necessary to stand in front of hundreds of people to share your story—public speaking is not for everyone—I urge you to experiment with a variety of strategies to find what helps you get your mojo back.

However you choose to do it, making positive change in the world is absolutely worthwhile. This is confirmed by people who stop me frequently when I'm out and about. Even though they might not know my name, they recognize my face and white hair from all the publicity the trial received. They wave, smile, and pause as if they're unsure if they should speak to me or not, and then they thank me for my efforts. They may relay a story from their own experiences or share something wrong or inappropriate that happened to someone they know—their mother, sister, daughter, or friend. Most often, when I ask about the well-being of the target, I'm told they managed to pull through. Usually, it's because they made the tough choice to exit their situation and move on. It's a choice that no one wants to make, and it really doesn't feel like a choice at all. It's more like taking the path of least resistance. Unfortunately, the path of least resistance allows someone else—the perpetrator—to hold a position of power with no sense of remorse and zero accountability. It's not fair or even right, but it's reality.

That reality led me to think long and hard about the factors contributing to workplace harassment. How could I get to the bottom of the issue and find out the best way to stop it? There will always be jerks around who are willing to offend others, oblivious to the very real consequences of their actions. How can we prevent the heartache and emotional distress targets endure? For the most part, it depends upon employers. They're responsible for initiating tough conversations, providing educational mandates, and establishing policies to react to situations of harassment. Organizations either get it right or totally biff it. My employer missed numerous opportunities to educate staff, promote understanding, and change hearts and minds. I'm sharing my experiences so you can avoid them.

BROADER ADVOCACY

Continued change means reaching large numbers of people and showing them how to make a difference in small and meaningful ways. Leading others through open and honest discussions can create accountability and great workplaces. We need to continue thinking beyond our settings and circumstances.

Thinking "beyond" led me to a fruitful networking opportunity that broadened my personal mission's scope. Friends connected me to Sollah Interactive, LLC, a company that serves organizations by producing and selling training materials, including unique and market-disrupting content. The materials included engaging and unique training videos with accompanying follow-up and talking points. Sollah's action-oriented mindset fit with my approach to advocacy. Thinking outside the box and being open to new avenues of distribution could further my mission's reach.

I chose to work with Sollah because they offered unique, high quality videos that disrupt typical perspectives. They put the trainee in the decision-making seat instead of telling them what to do. They offer pointed follow-up questions, discussion points, and helpful tips and tricks, infusing individual accountability into everything produced. Their thought-provoking, empowering scenarios aren't typically portrayed in mainstream training, and I love that. This thought-provoking approach is one way to positively change the status quo.

By working with Sollah, I was able to build a new, solid relationship and share common goals with the training company production team. In fact, I co-produced a training video with them. As their subject matter expert on sexual harassment, I helped produce an amazing 10-minute presentation titled *I Said Something*. I'm very proud of the end product.

As the subject matter expert during the video recording session, I provided input and helped guide the actors' portrayals. I also served as the narrator. During the rehearsal of a brief monologue, a particularly talented actress brought her role to life. She portrayed her embarrassment about frequently being shamed by her boss in front of her coworkers. She was so shocked by an episode of public embarrassment that she refused to return to the office the next day.

Her portrayal brought tears to my eyes. For years, that was my experience. Her visceral depiction transported me into a familiar space of darkness, fear, and skepticism. In that moment, when I saw and felt my old emotions playing out through someone else, I knew others would see and feel it too. It would compel them to stand up themselves.

Producing that video gave me a key way to share my experience and educate others, to "pay it forward." Paying it forward is a great way to build confidence, find your voice and regain your power. There are so many ways to do it:

- Serve on a board to make change happen.

- Take an active role in your community on an issue you care about.

- Use your voice. Start a face-to-face dialogue with a willing participant.

- Join a committee or group that meets regularly to discuss a topic you're passionate about.

- Write a letter or make a phone call and start a discussion about the change you want to see in this world.

The ripple effect of your actions will extend farther than you think.

Paying it forward is also a way to find community and become a part of something bigger than yourself. Community creates an environment for connections, healing, and comradery, all of which are vitally important to a happy and decent life. It's transformative. Communities of all kinds are everywhere around us! The feminist community. The religious community. The gamer community. The cat-loving community. And of course, the sexually harassed target community. There is a community for everyone because we take comfort in finding that "sameness" in others. Paying it forward allows us to step out and meet others we might not otherwise cross paths with.

In 2018 with advocacy in mind, I gathered a number of like-minded, passionate people into a working group focused on ending workplace harassment. By simply asking who would be willing to join the effort, wonderfully committed people came into my life. We met roughly every other Friday for coffee. Although we had different backgrounds, jobs, and ages, there was one thing we all had in common: we all cared about ending workplace harassment. We simply got together, drank coffee, discussed what was going on in our worlds, and planned how we could make a difference. We accomplished a few things: We established the name, Safe Accountable Workplaces (SAW), settled on a logo, and worked with a few state legislators to introduce bills in both the Iowa House and Senate.

Ultimately, SAW stopped meeting when life's path took members in various directions and it became too hard to get together. I still talk to group members, though, and I'm lucky they're in my life. Safe Accountable Workplaces came together when my need for human connection and advocacy intersected.

You too, can work to discover a community right for you and be open to what it brings to your life.

MOVING FORWARD

Life moves on, people move on, and wounds are healed. A few years post-verdict I sit and reflect on where we are going as a society. I reflect on how far we have come collectively, who I used to be, and how far I have come personally. The old me pops up occasionally; she's negative, nasty, anxious, and distrustful, like many people. She is the doubtful voice continuously hissing in my ear that I push back and stifle.

We can be our own worst enemies. That's why we must also work to become our own greatest cheerleaders. I'm fortunate: I have family whom I'm close to who love and support all of my endeavors. I have friends who cheer me on in all sorts of ways. I have a roof over my head, clothes on my back, and food on my table. My home life is stable, and I have a good relationship with God. These are all things I don't take lightly as I see so much hurt, anger, resentment, and strife in the world. My support systems helped me become a cheerleader for myself and pass on my strengths to others. This empowerment renewed my self-confidence and eventually allowed me to return to activities I had previously enjoyed, like politics.

After my dramatic ouster from the Statehouse, I was sure I'd never be involved with politics again. I grew up in a family full of Democrats. My parents stressed the beauty of democracy, and the freedoms that come with it, especially the importance of voting. They took my brother and I with them to the polling station whenever there was a choice to be made for something or someone.

My views about politics changed as my perspective broadened with maturity and life experience. My views are different. I'd like to think I'm more aware of reality, of how harsh life can be for many. My views are more open, optimistic, and caring toward others. I've learned the importance of awareness, of knowing how my actions impact others. The decisions that any of us make can potentially have repercussions well into the future whether we like it or not. So think about your decisions carefully.

I'm content with the tough decisions I made. I have no regrets. I don't think about what would have happened had I not come forward to speak my truth. Why look back when the path forward is so interesting? For me, moving forward and coming forward was worth it. Not everyone can come forward, for reasons already discussed. We have to respect that. We have to judge a lot less and respect a little more.

In a world that shoves respect aside for judgement and bias, we have to do a better job at bucking the system and extending respect more freely. It will benefit everyone in the long run. I cannot wait until the day I turn on the news to hear a report that declares workplace harassment to be an antiquated concept, that incidents, civil cases, and settlements are down to single-digit percentages, or better yet no longer required.

This book will help you tip the scales of justice in that direction. I hope hearing my truth serves as inspiration for you. May it empower you to find your voice, speak your truth, and regain your power. What you say and do matters. And it can change the world.

HOPE

> "Hope is one of the principal springs that keep mankind in motion."
>
> – Thomas Fuller

HOPE IS ALL around us. It's in my son's eyes as I happily watch his excitement in a new experience. It's in my yard as green grass sprouts up from the cold, brown earth every spring. It's in the books we read as we eagerly turn a page, waiting for the next sentence. Hope is all around us. We simply have to look for it.

Writing these sentences in the midst of a worldwide pandemic made me see the vital importance of hope in our lives. It made me aware of its foundational presence during our healing journeys and as an integral part of our psyches in a world filled with divisiveness and polarization.

Hope is alive and well and more important than ever.

I started writing this book at a time when worldwide tensions were high and world leaders were flexing muscles of oppression. Harassment and bullying were front and center thanks to social media and our culture's appetite for drama. Society was beginning to recognize the widespread damage done by bullies with a national pulpit. The act of speaking truth to power was taking hold, instilling newfound confidence in people.

I finished writing this book in the midst of a worldwide pandemic where pervasive uncertainty looms large. A lot changed in the span of three months, changed again in the next three months, then changed yet again in three more months. The one thing that remained steady despite the change was hope. Hope for normalcy, hope for resiliency, hope for sanity!

The world quickly transformed into chaos. People were dying from a mysterious illness. Suddenly workplaces all over the globe were temporarily closed or their functions altered in some way. Others were shuttered for good. Almost every business adapted to a new, unstable reality to protect people from an invisible assailant. Working on this book became much more than simply a recovery story. This book, which aims to help people in any type of workplace, became more daunting than I anticipated. As the world changed, so did my emotional range and my resolve to finish it. I wanted to help people do more than simply recover; I wanted them to gain the mental strength to thrive in their own space and environment.

I kept coming back to hope and the idea that change is a constant in every life. Physical workplaces change all the time. They'll continue to change long after we leave this earth. Facing workplace challenges and developing the mental acuity we need at any given time to become nimbler will help us face any situation. By normalizing tough conversations, addressing issues head-on, fostering more dialogue, and simply thinking differently we will not only keep hope alive but change the construct of workplaces for the better, whatever the future might be.

Lately, the term, "return to normalcy" has come into our periphery. I don't find it helpful; "normal" is simply not an option for so many. What is a normal workplace anymore? Who gets to dictate what "normal" means? My normal is different than yours, and that's okay.

What I do like is optimism and the fact that a worldwide pandemic has revealed many things about workplaces. Not every workplace needs people to gather together within four walls to get the job done. Productivity may increase without traditional workplace distractions. On the other hand, for some, a workplace creates a space for socialization. It provides respite from an undesirable or stressful homelife. Thank goodness we have been enlightened by the good, bad, and ugly of so many situations. Pandemic or no, unless addressed, the fundamental issues in a workplace won't cease to exist simply because four walls are changed. That's why this book is important at any time. Because it's less about an actual workplace and more about the person who is reading this and what they choose to do with the information.

One day, when a "return to normalcy" is referenced, it will mean employees are able to work in an environment free from stress, fear, shame, and guilt. They'll be in a place that allows them to comfortably and confidently contribute to their work organization. One day, we will live in a harassment-free world.

ACKNOWLEDGEMENTS

FIRST AND FOREMOST, I want to thank my amazing husband, Jeff, for his unwavering support and encouragement, even when I was hard to live with. Thank you to Ewan, who reminded me when he was six, "Mom, you're a lady; you can do anything," and for challenging me in the best ways. To my mom and dad, Jeff and Linda Anderzhon, who taught me well and continue to go above and beyond as friends and supporters.

To Deborah Froese, my editor, for going on this book journey with me and teaching me a lot and bringing out what I didn't even know I needed in this book. I'm eternally grateful.

Thank you, Paige Glidden, for recognizing in 1998 that we'd be better as best friends than rivals. I love us! Nicole Smith, your steadfast, unrelenting friendship sustains me. Kerry Wise, for more than 20 years of energy, support and realism that keeps me going. To Sarah Clark, whose faith and enthusiasm inspire me. To Susan Judkins Josten for being my mentor and always helping me focus on what's right and true.

To Michael Carroll, for always having my back. Thank you for knowing just what to say to me and when to say it. What started as a business partnership is now a life-changing, enduring friendship.

And finally, to Jan, who has been with me from the beginning and has seen and heard it all. Thank you for continuing to cheer me on behind the scenes. I value and appreciate you.

RESOURCES

THIS SECTION LISTS organizations that provide reputable information and life-changing services for those seeking support in their search for healing and justice. Seek resources that work for you and your situation, including those at a local level. To help you find local resources, a number of keyword searches are included at the bottom of this list. The internet offers a vast array of information to suit any narrative or agenda, so please verify the reputation, content, and contact information of any group or organization you find online.

AMERICAN COUNSELING ASSOCIATION

Find a licensed counseling professional in your area with their online Therapy Directory database.

6101 Stevenson Ave., Suite 600
Alexandria, VA 22304
1-800-347-6647
www.counseling.org

KINDNESS.ORG

Through science and education, this online organization inspires others to make a kinder world, one act at a time.

NATIONAL ASSOCIATION FOR THE ADVANCEMENT OF COLORED PEOPLE (NAACP)

This historic organization is the pre-eminent civil rights group in the nation.

National Headquarters
4805 Mt. Hope Drive
Baltimore MD 21215
Toll Free: (877) NAACP-98 (877-622-2798)
www.naacp.org

NATIONAL ORGANIZATION FOR WOMEN

Founded in 1966, this organization recognizes the importance of ending violence, abuse and harassment against all women.

www.now.org

NATIONAL WOMEN'S LAW CENTER

This organization employs experts who fight for gender justice: "We drive change in the courts, public policy, and in our society, especially for women facing multiple forms of discrimination."

11 Dupont Circle, NW, #800
Washington, DC 20036
P: 202-588-518
Legal Help: 202-319-3053
www.nwlc.org

PROJECT HAPPINESS GLOBAL

This online nongovernmental organization studies and provides insight on happiness as well as daily and weekly inspiration.

https://projecthappiness.org

RAINN (RAPE, ABUSE & INCEST NATIONAL NETWORK)

RAINN offers crisis support information and services twenty-four hours a day, seven days a week.

1-800-656-HOPE (4673)

www.rainn.org

SOCIETY OF HUMAN RESOURCE MANAGEMENT

The Society for Human Resource Management creates better workplaces where employers and employees thrive together. SHRM has chapters throughout the country.

1-800-283-SHRM (7476)

www.shrm.org

SUBSTANCE ABUSE AND MENTAL HEALTH ADMINISTRATION (SAMSHA) HELP HOTLINE

SAMSHA, a division of the US Department of Health and Human Services, has hotlines accessible 24 hours a day, seven days a week.

1-800-662-HELP (4357)

www.samhsa.gov/find-help/national-helpline

TIME'S UP FOUNDATION

TIME'S UP approaches "safe, fair, and dignified work" from various angles to support, empower, and educate survivors.

TIME'S UP Foundation
PO Box 33633
1800 M Street, NW
Washington, DC 20033
www.timesupfoundation.org

UN WOMEN

A United Nations entity dedicated to gender equality and the empowerment of women, UN Women is a global champion for women and girls. It was established to accelerate progress on meeting their needs worldwide.

www.unwomen.org

UNITED STATES EQUAL EMPLOYMENT OPPORTUNITY COMMISSION (EEOC)

The US EEOC enforces federal laws that make it illegal to discriminate against a job applicant or an employee because of the person's race, color, religion, sex (including pregnancy, transgender status, and sexual orientation), national origin, age (40 or older), disability or genetic information.

www.eeoc.gov

WORKPLACE BULLYING INSTITUTE

Just like the name suggests, this organization researches and educates the public about workplace bullying.

https://workplacebullying.org/

9 TO 5, NATIONAL ASSOCIATION OF WORKING WOMEN

Today, 9 to 5 is one of the largest, most respected national membership organizations of working women in the US, dedicated to putting working women's issues on the public agenda.

http://www.9to5.org/

KEYWORD SEARCHES

"Harassment support services near me"

"Confidence building activities"

"Harassment counseling services near me"

"Assault and abuse help near me"

"Dealing with bullies at work"

"How to begin emotional healing"

"Gender equality near me"

"My workplace rights"

"Stories of hope"

ENDNOTES

1   "2018 Study on Sexual Harassment and Assault," *Stop Street Harassment,* published February 1, 2018, https://stopstreetharassment.org/our-work/nationals-tudy/2018-national-sexual-abuse-report/.

2   *Merriam Webster Dictionary*, accessed March 15, 2021, https://www.merriam-webster.com/dictionary/victim.

3   *Google Dictionary* accessed March 28, 2021, *https://www.google.com/search/target.*

4   Kathleen J. Mullen and Jeffrey B. Wenger, "Many Americans Face Bullying, Harassment and Abuse at Work, but Bosses Can Help," Rand Corporation, The Rand Blog, published August 30, 2017, https://www.rand.org/blog/2017/08/many-americans-face-bullying-harrassment-and-abuse.html.

5   Chai R. Feldblum and Victoria A. Lipnic, "Select Task Force on the Study of Harassment in the Workplace," U.S. Equal Employment Opportunity Commission, published June 2016, https://www.eeoc.gov/eeoc/task_force/harassment/report.cfm.

6   *U.*S. Equal Employment Opportunity Commission, "Sexual Harassment," accessed March 21, 2021, https://www.eeoc.gov/laws/types/sexual_harassment.cfm.

7   Arindrajit Dube, Eric Freeman, and Michael Reich, "Employee Replacement Costs," Berkeley University, Institute for Research on Labor and Employment, published March 4, 2010, https://irle.berkeley.edu/files/2010/Employee-Replacement-Costs.pdf.

8   Zanny Minton Beddoes, Editor-in-Chief, "Measuring the #MeToo Backlash," *The Economist*, published October 18, 2018, https://www.economist.com/united-states/2018/10/20/measuring-the-metoo-backlash.

9   Jessica Stillman, "Most Annoying Study Ever Says Bullying Is Good for Job Security," *Inc.,* July 23, 2014, https://www.inc.com/jessica-stillman/most-annoying-study-ever-says-bullying-is-good-for-job-security.html.

10   "Top Sales Executive Salary in the United States," Salary.com, accessed April 13, 2021, https://www.salary.com/research/salary/benchmark/top-sales-executive-salary.

11   Stephen Miller, "Average Entry Level Salary of for Recent College Grads Hovers Near $51,000," the Society for Human Resource Management (SHRM), August 22, 2019, https://www.shrm.org/resourcesandtools/hr-topics/compensation/pages/average-starting-salary-for-recent-college-grads.aspx.

12   David Goguen, "How, and How Much, Do Lawyers Charge?" Lawyers.com, updated July 23, 2020, https://www.lawyers.com/legal-info/research/how-and-how-much-do-lawyers-charge.html.

13   Minna J. Kotkin, "Outing Outcomes: An Empirical Study of Confidential Employment," Page 111 (or 1 of the PDF), 2007, http://law2.wlu.edu/deptimages/Law%20Review/64-1%20Kotkin%20Article.pdf

14   This quote has been credited to a few people from Plato and Socrates to Ian Maclaren.

15   Chai R. Feldblum and Victoria A. Lipnic, "Select Task Force on the Study of Harassment in the Workplace," U.S. Equal Employment Opportunity Commission, June 2016, https://www.eeoc.gov/eeoc/task_force/harassment/report.cfm.

16   Tarana Burke, "Inception," Me Too Movement, accessed March 21, 2021, https://metoomvmt.org/get-to-know-us/history-inception/.

17   U.S. Equal Employment Opportunity Commission, "Charges Alleging Sex-Based Harassment (Charges filed with EEOC) FY 2010 - FY 2020," U.S. Equal Employment Opportunity Commission, accessed March 21, 2021, https://www.eeoc.gov/eeoc/statistics/enforcement/sexual_harassment_new.cfm.

18   "October is Change the Culture Month in Iowa," Office of the Governor of Iowa, October 5, 2018, https://governor.iowa.gov/2018/10/october-is-change-the-culture-month-in-iowa.

19   "RAINN Hotline Helps Record Number of Survivors," RAINN (Rape, Abuse & Incest National Network), October 1, 2018, https://www.rainn.org/news/rainn-hotline-helps-record-number-survivors.

20   Matt Wynn and John Fritze, "Analysis: Trump more negative, prolific on Twitter amid Democratic impeachment inquiry," USA Today, December 23, 2019, https://www.usatoday.com/in-depth/news/politics/2019/12/23/donald-trumps-tweets-get-negative-impeachment-2020-election-loom/2601246001/.

21   Prakash Gangdev, "Forgiveness: A note for psychiatrists," *Indian Journal of Psychiatry*, Apr-Jun, 2019, Vol. 2, pg. 153–156, https://www.ncbi.nlm.nih.gov/pmc/articles/PMC2755173/.

22   Prakash Gangdev, "Forgiveness: A note for psychiatrists," *Indian Journal of Psychiatry*, Apr-Jun, 2019, Vol. 2, pg. 153–156.

23   Kathy Obradovich, "Senate leader Dix needs to step down; 'That was a sad display of leadership,' Anderson says," *Des Moines Register*, November 14, 2017, https://www.desmoinesregister.com/story/opinion/columnists/kathie-obradovich/2017/11/14/bill-dix-step-down-disastrous-news-conference-sex-harassment-case/864456001/.